OF MY HEART

THE CONTEMPORARY CHRISTIAN'S GUIDE TO ENJOYING THE
GOD KIND OF LIFE WITHOUT THE RULES OF RELIGION

KELLY PRICE

PUBLICATIONS
HOUSTON, TEXAS

Copyright ©2006   Kelly Price

All rights reserved. No part of this book may be reproduced or utilized in any manner or by any means, electronic or mechanical, including photocopying, recording, or by any information storage or retrieval system, without the expressed written permission of the publisher. Printed in the United States of America. Inquiries should be sent to the publisher at: Kelly Price, P.O. Box 80997, Conyers, GA 30013 or via e-mail at dearkelly@kellyprice.info

PUBLISHING CONSULTANTS
Renew Publications • P.O. Box 670321 • Houston, Texas 77267

PHOTOGRAPHY CREDITS—Pastor Sally Riley
COVER DESIGN—Preashea Hilliard
TYPESET AND DESIGN—Facelift Graphics

Manufactured in the United States of America

ISBN 0-9778256-0-4

THE GIFT OF MY HEART

In recent times I have learned the true meaning of the verse of scripture that says *"In everything give thanks to the Lord for this is the will of God in Christ Jesus concerning you"* (ITHESSALONIANS 5:18). As I am writing, I am in the process of receiving a spiritual promotion, just as many of you who sit and read these words right now are in the midst of moving to your next dimension in life.

These words, these thoughts, my secrets. They are all things that have been inscribed in my heart. They are eternally etched there through experiences and revelation. Some of the experiences were good, some were not so good, and many were really bad. But they all helped to bring forth lessons and revelation that God would have me to learn for the making of me, and the edifying of you.

My earnest desire is that you will receive the gifts of my heart. That you will receive it in the spirit that I give it to you and that you would, without hesitation, delve into the thoughts of my heart that I will share with you, and ultimately allow them to help you grasp the importance of this critical time you are in, why you must go through what you are going through, and why you must go through it with praise in your mouth and a song in your heart.

Learn from what they say and you will be blessed. These are the Inscriptions of My Heart.

PEACE & BLESSINGS,
KP

DEDICATION

To my husband Jeffery, my loudest cheerleader, my biggest fan and my greatest supporter. You constantly remind me that what the world gives is temporal and what God gives is eternal. The best is yet to come, you are the best and the world has yet to see YOU.

To my two beautiful children, Jeff, Jr. and Jonia, whose expectation of me causes me to continuously look to God for more strength when I feel like I can't go on. Because you are, I must be, I must do, and I must achieve so you will always know that through Christ all things are possible and in Him you also will be, will do, and will achieve. Mommy loves you.

THANK YOU

To God, who is not only the author and finisher of my faith, but is truly the author of this book.

To my Fathers and Mothers in the Gospel…
And to all of the men and women of God who have consistently spoken life into my life, including:

    Bishop Jerome and First Lady Joni Norman
    Pastor and Mrs. Charles Bonds
    Bishop Jasper and Lady Barbara Rolle
    Bishop Hilda Rolle
    Bishop and Mrs. Bobby Henderson
    Prophet and Lady Corey Easterling
    Bishop Joseph and Prophetess Edna Brown
    Pastor Donnie McClurkin
    Prophet Charles and Lady Virginia Buchanen
    Prophetess Carolyn Morgan
    Pastor Judy Shaw
    Prophet Todd Hall
    Pastor and Mrs. Willie Robinson, Sr.
    Bishop Frank and Dr. Juliette White
    Pastors Ricky and Vicky Walker
    The late Bishop Walter and Lady Dianne Bogan
    Pastor Kevin Williams
    The late Apostle Joseph Sims and Pastor Bea Sims
    Bishop and Mrs. Darryl Brister
    Prophet Bobby Brown
    Drs. I.V and Bridget Hilliard

INTRODUCTION

As I sit and begin to write this book, it is not reluctantly but it is with mixed emotions. It is not with some great outline, syllabus or plan that I begin this awesome task, but simply in obedience to the voice of the Lord that said "Write." For some time now, there has been a deep desire within me to write the sentiments of my heart. Furthermore the Word of the Lord has come many times in the last couple of years saying, "Write the books." However, there was always something to stop it. I was recording, promoting or touring and there was just not enough time. The truth was that although I could sit, and with a reasonable amount of eloquence, put my feelings, thoughts and experiences on paper, there was still something deep inside me that made me believe that I couldn't address the people. I had a little bit of the "I'm unworthy" thing going on. I told myself that people wouldn't hear what I had to say. They wouldn't receive me as a child of God. They'd wonder, "What makes her an authority? What gives her the right?" But one Friday evening in August 2004, as I was getting dressed for service, I heard the voice of the Lord say to me again as He had many times before, "Write". Ironically this would be at one of the most challenging times of my life and it just didn't make much sense, not now anyway. So I asked Him, "Write about what? I don't have anything to say right now and what I do have to say, I'm sure You don't want me to say (I thank God that He allows me to be me, totally honest about the way I feel)." And without delay, I heard His voice say to me again, "Write". It wasn't loud but it was stern and unwavering and I knew He meant it. Kind of like a child when your parent would tell you to do something. He didn't have to yell, there was just something in His tone and you know you'd better comply. So I said, "Okay Lord I will write, but I don't have anything to say. I don't know what to say or where to begin, but in obedience to You, I will sit at my computer after church tonight and wait for You to give me something."

Service let out very late this particular night. I guess this was because it was a revival and there was not one, but two prophets ministering under the anointing

AND it was a Friday night (I believe the timekeeper must have been relieved of his/her duties). However, I sat through the service and, because of what had transpired between me and God at home before I went to church, I expected some type of word or instruction to be given to me from the mouth of one of the prophets but in this particular service, as fiery as it was, there was no word of personal prophecy for me.

So after service, with no instruction on what it was that I should write about, I headed home. It was very late - or shall I say early - when I arrived home and I was exhausted from the long day I'd had, but I was sincere in my heart about what I told the Lord before leaving for service and I was going to honor it. So, I prepared myself to write. I set up my laptop in my bedroom and as the house quieted and the children settled into their usual it's-Friday-night-so-I'm-gonna-watch-TV-in-the-den-all-night-long-because-there-is-no-school-tomorrow positions, I sat down just as I'd promised I'd do and turned the computer on.

As I was obedient, God was faithful and the blank page that I pulled up with my Microsoft Word program did not remain blank very long. But as I was obedient, God did a miraculous thing. He took my weary mind and quickened it and as I laid my hands to the keys of my laptop I felt an anointing come over me and I could hear the Lord speak clearly as to what I was to write. I am very familiar with what the anointing to write feels like, as I have been blessed to have it overtake me regularly since the age of seven when I wrote my first song. There was something different about it this time. When I write music, something special happens because the song will sing itself to me and I can hear it in full orchestration with every drum kick, vocal arrangement, bass lick and cymbal crash in its proper place - but this was not a song. In the past I have even sat down to write memoirs that will eventually become parts of books that I've yet to publish and I've done that under the unction and leading of the Holy Ghost. But this wasn't that either. This time the Lord did something different, He did something special. This was new and I knew it. I could feel it. He wanted to let me know that even in this time of great challenge and trial in my life, His hand was on me, His spirit was with me and because of my faithfulness, there was a new level of anointing that was about to overtake me. I'd been seeking God for it through prayer and consecration, but this was my time and what I'd been after spiritually was due me at that moment. So not in a church service, tarry service, or some other form of public organized worship was my new anointing released to me. But because of a sincere heart and a kept promise, in the quiet of my bedroom in the middle of the night, I heard His words and felt the Spirit of the Lord endow me with power to reveal His word to His children. God favored me with the testimony of Elijah, who in his time of weariness, waited in the mountains and looked to hear from God. While in the mountains, Elijah witnessed great moves of God (just as I had in the service earlier that evening) in the form of winds, earthquakes, and fire. But God didn't speak to him through any of that. These were all amazing and wondrous acts of God, and surely He was in those acts, but once all the hoopla, excitement and demonstration was over, Elijah still needed to hear from God for his circumstance. Just like me sitting in that church and just like many of you reading this right now. For every time you go to a service and see great wonders and witness miracles and prophecy, and experience great praise and worship, after a while it all becomes hoopla, excitement and demonstration if you cannot or do not hear personally and directly from God for your circumstance. But look at what the Lord did for Elijah. There came a still small voice and Elijah heard what he needed to hear - which was instruction from the Father. And as God favored Elijah to hear, He favored me. Not only did I hear but I began to see visions of the things He spoke to me. The things that He has inscribed on my heart for years and years began to gush forth from me like a geyser and pretty soon my mind was going much faster than my hands. My typing skills (or lack thereof) couldn't keep up with all of the things that were breaking forth in the spirit sitting in my bedroom in the early hours of that morning. Because of this visitation, writing this book felt effortless, and before I realized it I looked up and it was nearly 5:00 am! WHAT A MIGHTY GOD WE SERVE!

I was so excited I had to force myself to lie down that morning and get some sleep so I would be able to get through the tasks of my Saturday. I knew this was a God thing and all of my inhibitions and insecurities went out the window. I promised the Lord as I lay in the bed, before I closed my eyes to sleep, that no matter what happened with my day I would make sure not to let one day go by that I wouldn't sit at the computer to write - even if it were just a few sentences. As I keep my writing covenant with the Father, as He unctions me, He faithfully meets me at my computer and gives me what to say.

AN UNLIKELY CANDIDATE

When I think about my first thoughts of doing this, I am reminded of Moses. He felt that he couldn't go before Pharaoh to free the children of Israel. After all who would listen to him? Pharaoh was king and he was a commoner. Not only was Moses a commoner, but in the eyes of Pharaoh he was a traitor, an ingrate who was raised in his home and given the best of everything the world had to offer, yet he walked away from it all to associate himself with slaves. And to top it all off, Moses had a speech impediment and stuttered when he spoke! Needless to say, he wasn't the most welcome sight in the house of Pharaoh and in the eyes of men, I'm sure Moses wasn't viewed as the most qualified for the job. But the Lord commanded Moses to go and instructed him, "If they ask who sent you tell them I AM THAT I AM sent you." So comes this book and those which you have not read from me yet. Not because of anything that I believe I can say or any influence I believe I would have, but simply because the Father, I AM THAT I AM, sends me and says, "Give the people what I have put in you." And with that, I have a charge to keep and a God to glorify, and I must do the will of Him who sends me.

PURPOSE

I must also acknowledge that writing these things have also ministered to me, which is a familiar thing. God has given me songs about love, life, marriage - the good and the bad sides of it - praise and pretty much any topic you can cover. Without fail, my songs would minister to me first and this was my indicator that

I had done what the Lord said even if the music industry didn't get it. I always knew it would be alright and God always gave me a witness. Hundreds and thousands of letters would come to me and people would pour their hearts out about how they felt I'd been right there with them going through the worst time of their life. They'd say, "If I could've expressed myself musically or even just with spoken words, the very things you said would've been what I would have said."

This is an experience that no matter how many times it happens to me my heart goes out, my soul gets lifted and I am completely humbled. Many times I will cry. I know that there are millions of hurting people all over the world - many of who feel like they are all alone. It is time to reach out and touch them where they are.

There is a great misunderstanding in people right now and much of it exists within the church. People don't resent God and they don't not want Him. They resent religion. They can't stand rules that banish them to Hell and have nothing to do with the condition of their soul. They hate coming to church and feeling like they aren't good enough because their clothes are different or their hair is different or the part of town that they are from is undesirable. They don't want to come to the place where unconditional love supposedly abounds, and because they have tattoos or multiple body piercings, they are ostracized and treated like aliens from another planet! The church is supposed to be a place for those who need it to be able to get help and healing. Somewhere along the line there has been a wrong turn and a great majority of our churches stopped transforming lives and ministering to souls and started molding "mini-me's" and doppelgangers. Thus we have come into a time where our churches are filled with clones. They look like the real thing and walk and talk like the real thing but closer investigation will reveal that they are clones with a form of Godliness and no power.

In many places, we have turned the church into a glorified country club - "Members Only" with preferred seating and parking and Sunday is our weekly visitor's day. This is the day we allow people to come in, walk around, feel us out and see if they want to join our club – while at the same time, we are deciding whether we want them in our club. Those who feel welcomed join and others, who don't, don't. Some join then slowly slack off and eventually stop coming because they are not made to feel like they are a part of the family.

DUAL CITIZENSHIP

As the daughter of two sanctified Church of God in Christ preachers, raised under the leadership of my Bishop granddaddy, I was inundated with more church responsibility by the time I was 12 than many of you will ever have in your lifetime. I went from being a background vocalist for the industry's top selling artists to becoming a noted songwriter and platinum selling R&B artist myself. I have had the opportunity to experience the good and the bad side of both places. I have lived life with dual citizenship. I know what it is to walk into a church and be placed under the microscope and scrutinized the entire time. I've heard the whispers. "What is she doing here? Is that the R&B singer?" If it wasn't the asking for an autograph, it was the onsite audition for the aspiring young singer whose mama would then get angry and tell me I was stuck up because I wouldn't listen. All I wanted was for someone to see through me and know that I was broken and crying out for help.

I often felt pulled to just please the people in those instances, but God was very specific with me and there were boundaries and rules that came along with this territory. I was never to take my celebrity status into the church and do anything to bring more attention to myself than what would already be brought to me by others. It wasn't always easy because making people happy was the biggest part of my job. That's what artists are - they are pacifiers to the masses, many times at the expense of their own peace. Sometimes people would understand and sometimes they wouldn't and when they didn't, they were cruel and said nasty things - often right there in the church. So although I made an effort to stay connected to the church, many times I'd leave services feeling worse than when I came because I needed to receive and would find myself being pulled on and sucked dry from what was already a nearly depleted source.

I wanted the God of my youth and I couldn't come and get Him because church people were blocking the road.

So through much emotional see-sawing and what has been a long road back from bitterness, anger and depression, I have been restored and commissioned to go and do for those who are living what God allowed me to live and understand. Through my own personal encounters, I know that there is a peace that has eluded society for so long that many have given up on ever knowing what real peace is. God has given me a gift and I realize now that it's more than just music. My experiences were not just for me. I had to go through much of what I've been through to be a relational tool of witness for the kingdom in a time when people will not hear just anyone. They need to know that you relate. They want proof that you understand where they've been and who they are because you are who they are and you've been where they are now. I am grateful because it is something that allows me to not only touch people from all walks of life, but to feel them as well.

It is my prayer that, through this offering to the world, those who are facing difficulties in their Christianity will gain strength and those who have been confused or turned-off by religion will see that having a true relationship with the Lord has nothing to do with religion.

You are His beloved and His chosen child. He wants you to know Him personally and intimately and He wants you to experience life as you have never imagined.

CONTENTS

SECTION I - PRAYER: POWER AND PITFALLS

CHAPTER 1 Prayer 16
CHAPTER 2 Prayer and Fasting 21
CHAPTER 3 His Will or Your Answer? 33
CHAPTER 4 Watch Your Mouth! 38
CHAPTER 5 Words Have Life, Words Are Life 41
CHAPTER 6 The Power of Speaking Words vs 46
The Power of Speaking a Word
CHAPTER 7 The Words of My Mouth 53

SECTION II - FAITH: YOU'VE GOT IT!

CHAPTER 8 Divine Healing or Doctor's Healing? 60
CHAPTER 9 The Fear Factor 67
CHAPTER 10 The Truth About Faith 79
CHAPTER 11 You're Pregnant With a Promise! 85

SECTION III - PRAISE: FOR LIFE

CHAPTER 12 Anointed to Praise 92
CHAPTER 13 Praise=Energy, Energy=Praise 93
CHAPTER 14 The David Connection 97
CHAPTER 15 There is Freedom in Your Praise 102
CHAPTER 16 A Cold Blooded Praise 109
CHAPTER 17 The Dictation of Praise 121
CHAPTER 18 Your Son, David, The Shepherd 128
CHAPTER 19 Praise Comes From Your Private Places 133
CHAPTER 20 Profile of a Praiser 138

CONTENTS

SECTION IV - THE ABUNDANT LIFE

CHAPTER 21 The Qualifications For Total Life Prosperity 144

CHAPTER 22 The Parable of The Amusement Park 147

CHAPTER 23 Change The Way You Think 152

CHAPTER 24 Survivor or Overcomer? 157

CHAPTER 25 All or Nothing 164

CHAPTER 26 The Microwave Mentality 167

CHAPTER 27 Slow Cooked Sanctification 173

CHAPTER 28 Let's Get Naked!! 178

CHAPTER 29 Be The Best 183

SECTION I
Prayer: Power and Pitfalls

PRAYER

What is prayer? Webster's Dictionary defines prayer as *an address (as a petition) to God in word or thought; an earnest request or wish.*

I like to define prayer as *an intense and personal or intimate conversation or communing between God and man, usually initiated by man.*

PRAYER IS COMMON

We all pray, or have prayed at some point in our lives. It is so common that sometimes we pray and don't even realize we are praying. Like the occasion where you are in the street and not looking too fresh and you see a gentleman you know and find quite attractive. You are scrambling because you are between weaves and you look a hot mess! Before you realize it you're whispering, "Oh Lord, please don't let him see me!" You've just said a prayer and didn't even realize it! Now although that really wasn't a prayer as you'd intend for prayer to be, it was in fact a prayer because you addressed the Lord and made a request.

By the way - God doesn't answer those kinds of prayers. That situation comes under the categories of common sense and things you can do yourself (like your hair!). So please don't pray that one anymore, okay? And if you embarrass that easily, don't leave the house looking that way!

That example was comical and maybe a little to the left, but I want you to see how precious prayer is and why it shouldn't be wasted on meaningless things.

Prayer is often taken for granted or even misused as it was in the example I just gave. How many times has this been you?

THE LAST RESORT
Now think of the times in your life when you, without a doubt, acknowledge and respect the power of prayer in the life of the believer. Think of the times when you needed someone to pray for you or you broke down and decided to pray. Think of more than one occasion and I'm sure you'll see the same look on your face in each instance. Trouble. It is these moments when you after trying everything your own way are broken down enough to call on God and cry out for help. It is at these times when we, after much consideration, find ourselves very willingly doing what our extremely hectic lives usually don't leave time for us to do - and that is pray!

But why put yourself through all that emotional turbulence? Why always wait until you have exhausted every other possibility before coming to Jesus with your needs? The truth is, if you go over your life He is the only one who never failed you. Even when times got to their absolute worst and you may have wanted to die - God said NO! And rather than giving up on you when you wanted to give up on yourself, He continued to breathe life into you and force you to face your days until such a time that you would bend your will to His and ask Him to change you and change your life. Now you see that there is great destiny in you. Now you know that you will not die until you achieve it.

We have learned that there is power in the tongue. Death and life at the most extreme points of that power. We have also learned that the power of the tongue rests in every man and woman who has walked the Earth before you. That power rests in the mouth of every man and woman who now walks the Earth with you. This ability is given to everyone; however, corruption in the minds of humans has tainted this delicate gift.

But if I have this ability, why not just rely on the power of the tongue? If I can get what I want by just speaking it, why pray? Because remember, and you will see this more than once in this book, the ability to speak words and assign them to a person's life or destiny is common and without good or Godly intentions, it becomes carnal, soulish and selfish. But prayer - unlike speaking words - can only work in the lives of those who have relationship with the Father.

Before moving any further, I must say that if the stigma of using prayer just to get something from God can be broken, then we will come to understand it for what it was truly meant to be in the life of God's children. As a person with the true understanding of the nature of prayer, you will always see greater results than someone else who just prays. There is a secret to prayer.

THE SECRET OF PRAYER

Obtaining the secret to prayer is not a difficult task. Rather it is quite simple indeed. Prayer was designed so that the believer could commune on a greater level of intimacy with the Creator. Everyone prays at some time but not everyone can reach a place of communing through prayer. Intimacy and communing through prayer. That is the secret! The Lord wants to talk with us regularly. Not just when we need something, want something, or, are in trouble. Sadly, many only pray in those three specific instances. Then the believer - or Christian, as we like to call ourselves - who does pray more frequently, finds himself rushing through prayer because he has so much else to do. All God wants is some dedicated time for just you and Him. Think about your relationship with your spouse. When you first started dating there was excitement in getting to know them. Every date or encounter was a new adventure and you told all your friends about your new boyfriend or girlfriend. There were times when you would get on the telephone and end up talking all night long and not even realizing how much time had passed until you saw daylight creeping through your window. Although you had work or class, you didn't mind because that was your Boo! Every night you would sit and talk and even when you were exhausted you'd sit on the phone and just listen to each other breathe and fall asleep together and wake up together, but there was nothing perverted or impure about it, you just didn't want to let go. This is the secret. It's right there, built into you, because God put it there.

The only way He could get you to understand how He wants love between you and Him was to give you a visible, tangible example and that is through the purity of true love designed for a marriage relationship that a man and woman share. But God wants it all, just like you do! Now that you are in relationship with God, you don't have those all-night conversations with Him anymore. You don't brag about Him to your friends, coworkers and family. You don't bring anyone to meet Him anymore. Spiritually, you are walking around in an oversized, faded, terry cloth robe with curlers in your hair and Noxzema on your face! Not cute. What has taken His place in your heart? Is He no longer the love of your life?

In another chapter in this book I talk about God's emotions for us being the source from which we get our emotions. The Bible tells us that God is a jealous God and that He will share His glory with no other. Not just the glory of His works or His acts, but the glory of His creation. What is the glory of God's creation? MAN IS! When we make time for everything but Him, He gets jealous. When we reduce our prayers to the "gimme" and "I wanna" prayers because that's all we have time for - He is insulted. And He should be. When all you can do is ask and never make time for anything else, you push Him away and cause distance between you and Him. Think about it this way. How do you react when you see someone and you know every time they see you they are going to ask you for money? You may tolerate it for a little while, but when you get sick of it you are either going to give them a chunk of your mind or you are going to start avoiding them altogether. Why? Because you don't appreciate feeling like the only reason anyone wants to be around you is because they think you can do something for them. No one wants to be used. Well, what about God? After a while, you shouldn't even expect Him to meet you in prayer because it is no longer about the two of you, but rather about you and your needs. Sounds like a selfish lover to me! You wouldn't tolerate that behavior from your spouse, so why would you expect God to tolerate it from you?

It must be give and take. He wants you to take your time and talk to Him - tell Him the desires of your heart, tell Him how much you love Him. Tell Him you appreciate all that He's done for you and then listen to what He says in return. He wants to talk to you too. He wants to tell you He loves you too. He wants to show you what He desires for you and how He wants to make you happy, but you must make the time. He hasn't gone anywhere. He is still excited about you the way He was when you first met Him and He wants to "take it back" to those days. It is about relationship with God. It is about intimacy with your Heavenly Father. It is about communing with the greatest love of your life! That is the real secret to prayer. It is a secret but not a mystery. You have known it and had it all along. Now what are you gonna do about it?

Chapter Two
PRAYER AND FASTING

Prayer and fasting are spiritual tools that I was introduced to as a child through the lives of my mother and my grandparents. It sounds strange, maybe even mystical, to those who hear of it and don't know of its power from their own experience. I'll go as far as to say that I would have to agree had I not watched my whole life as impossible situations became possible as a result of prayer and fasting. But how can speaking words (praying) bring healing to a sick body? And how can not eating (fasting) or "turning down my plate" as the old saints would call it, prepare me for life's inevitable challenges?

First you must know that there are no great mysteries to be uncovered about praying and fasting where you are concerned. It starts out simply with your desire to draw closer to God, or your need to seek Him for specific answers to your life, and then your willingness to practice self-control and bring your SELF (your fleshly "must haves" such as food, sex, sleep or anything else you cannot say "no" to) under subjection in order to experience supernatural growth, and open and sincere communication with your Heavenly Father.

Prayer, its components and its effects are spoken of in so many places in this book. However, it is very difficult not to again bring up the necessity of it and what it stands for in the life of the believer, especially as it relates to fasting. Separately, prayer and fasting are each powerful weapons of warfare that are dominating forces in bringing victory into the life of the believer. However, when used together, they are the spiritual equivalent to weapons of mass destruction - everything in their path WILL BE destroyed! When you pray and seek God for an answer through prayer, you are telling Him first, "Lord, I have a situation and I need to talk to you about it because I cannot, will not, dare not make a move without consulting you because we are in relationship and I don't move without you." He loves this, because - as I have said and will say in other parts of this book - He wants to feel trust from you and although He already knows everything about you, it indulges Him to know that you value your relationship with Him so much that you would share the secrets of your heart and the challenges of your day. Think about it. When you come home at the end of your day there are times when all you want to do is just have your spouse, the closest person in the world to you, listen attentively as you tell of your wonderful or not so wonderful day. If they do not pay attention or validate the emotions associated with the things you share with them, you can become frustrated or aggravated, offended or even angered, at their lack of attentiveness and consideration for what is very pressing for you at that moment. We as God's children have that attentiveness available to us and we blatantly ignore it. Your Heavenly Father waits for you to come to Him daily. He wants to know, "Honey, how was your day?" and we won't talk to Him about it. Sounds like the spouse who comes home and slams doors and goes off in silence, ignoring the mate bearing a cool drink and a shoulder rub, grunting and complaining about not being bothered. Why? Because it's too much work, which brings me to the next point. Going to Him in prayer represents your willingness to labor for your answer. Why labor? Isn't prayer supposed to be an intimate conversation between the Father and His child? Yes, but in these instances, it is labor because there are times in our walk when - more often than not - we have to work to curb our natural instinct to murmur and complain or to try to fix things on our own. Fixing things on your own is labor, but going to God in prayer is labor of another kind. It is spiritual labor. You are literally "working" your flesh over and disciplining yourself to cultivate you relationship with the Lord rather than "going off" on someone or jumping on the phone and complaining to your friends so that you feel better. These are the times that - though they are most trying - are also your greatest opportunity for growth and spiritual promotion. But remember that even on your natural job, promotion goes to the one who the boss sees as the hardest working individual, the most diligent, the one who will stop at nothing to accomplish the task, fix the problem or get the answer. This is no different. It's work! That means sometimes you have to come in early - get out of the bed at 5:00 a.m. and labor before the Lord in prayer. Sometimes you have to work through lunch - fast. Then there are times you'll have to stay late and put in overtime - instead of praying for the 30 minutes you normally pray, stay on your knees until you feel something change.

FASTING. To *fast*, as recorded in Webster's New World Dictionary and Thesaurus is a verb meaning *to abstain from or to deny oneself of all or certain foods, not eat; to go hungry or simply to abstain*. A *fast*, used as a noun and according to the same reference tool, is *a period of abstaining*.

Fasting, to put it as plainly as I can, is a self-imposed starving for a spiritual purpose. Many people have adopted this practice as a means of protest or persuasion when they have petitions and are involved in often times publicly-known political or moral differences of opinion.

The true intention for fasting was, and still is, for the believer to impose a starving upon him or herself as a means of disciplining the flesh for a purpose or with an intended reason for a desired outcome. They seek to accomplish this by taking away its greatest pleasures so that nothing can distract them from hearing from God or so that God could be persuaded to favorably answer a petition that had been placed before Him by the believer.

Why fasting? Why something so drastic to get God's attention? When you fast, or impose hunger on yourself, you literally deny your body (your flesh) the very things it says it must have to survive. If the things your body or flesh needs to survive are being taken from it then the fact exists that after a period of time you (your flesh) will die.

Because of the practice of fasting being taken from its spiritual origin and being exploited and redefined for carnal purposes such as politics and other issues, people have believed that fasting is only associated with food. Fasting is a self-imposed starving of anything that your body (your flesh) craves. This means food AND sex. This also means, for those who didn't know, watching television and movies. For some of you it means talking on the phone and going shopping. It is anything that helps to keep your mind and your spirit polluted with non-spiritual things. For some this list of things is longer than others. It's personal. It's a sacrifice.

It is a time of HIGH CONSECRATION wherein you deny yourself the things you want the most. However, through this act of self-discipline, you are telling God, "I need to hear from You so badly" or "I want what You have for me so badly, that I literally would die for it!" For those of you who have fasted before, you can testify that it feels like you are dying. That is the very thing that lets you know that what you are doing is spiritual and that it is warfare. Your body (flesh) literally is fighting the will of your spirit with aches and pains to try and get you to give in to what it wants. You must know that it will pull out all the stops. The flesh will not play fair because it wants to be appeased and it wants to be in control. Think about it. You can get busy with your day - running errands, paying bills, shopping or doing whatever else your day calls for and get to the end of the day and realize you haven't eaten all day long, but never missed it. With that you will never even stop to complain of hunger or even get a headache or stomach cramp. But guess what? SORRY! You didn't fast, you just forgot to stop and eat. Why is this not a fast? Because it was not intentionally self-imposed and there was no purpose to it.

Now think about the times you have told yourself, "I am going to fast today." It seems like by 8:00 a.m. you are going to die - and you've only been awake since 7:00! This is not just you, but it is everyone! I have never been a breakfast person, even as a child. However, in my less spiritually mature days, every time I purposed in my heart to fast, I would wake up feeling like I hadn't eaten in three days! I would have headaches, moods swings and want to lie in bed all day long until it was over. Even now, there are times when I declare a fast or if the Lord puts me on a fast, I will wake up so hungry when any other time I can literally go all day and not think about food until I slow down. But again, this is how you know that what you are doing is spiritual and is heavy warfare.

But this is just the food element. What about the other things we must abstain from during a fast? What about sex? When you are forced to deny your body this pleasure because this time is being dedicated to the Lord – mind, body and spirit – it seems like it goes crazy! It even seems like the heat inside you of you is going to burn you up from the inside out - but we must learn to control our bodies and not let our bodies control us! Now, there are specific guidelines to fasting in the Bible that offer wisdom where it concerns abstaining from physical intimacies (of all kinds) and keeping your body, for those who are married (SEE I CORINTHIANS 7:3-5). For those who are not married, I don't address the abstaining while fasting because you should be abstaining at all times… that's another chapter in another book! As for those addicted to shopping and television and talking on the phone and other things, you must bring these under subjection and abstain from these things as well during periods of high consecration. You cannot sit on the phone half the day while consecrating. The reality of it is that when you are sitting on the phone that long, your conversation isn't going to stay on Jesus the whole time. During times of high consecration, you cannot sit and watch television or watch DVD's and movies. The two don't mesh. You cannot consecrate and commune with God while watching the plot in a movie unfold with a character making plans to move in deception to hide his/her sinful behavior. These images infiltrate your mind and feed your spirit at a time when it is most open and most vulnerable. Whether or not you realize it when you position yourself to fast and consecrate, you open your mind and spirit so whatever you bring to it or allow in its environment during this very sensitive time will attach to you and embed within you.

FASTING IS PERSONAL
Fasting is denying yourself everything that you have a hard time resisting on any given day. You know your personal temptations and your guilty pleasures. Because salvation is personal, this very important part of your walk with Christ is personal also. So we don't talk about fasting with everyone when we are doing it. We don't walk around looking like we are getting ready to faint from hunger. Instead we are to fight through the physical discomforts and push to get through our days as normally as we would any other day, not drawing attention to the fact that we are fasting.
SEE MATTHEW 6:16-18

Why? If this is a good thing, why not tell someone I'm doing it? Fasting is viewed as honorable whether it is by other Christians or even non-believers who understand the discipline associated with fasting. A common response to someone's knowledge of your fasting would be to ask what you are fasting for (that's personal and definitely shouldn't be discussed) or even to comment on how good you are that you can make yourself do that. When you talk about your fast as if it is the news of the day you have betrayed a trust between you and the Father. It is the equivalent to sharing an emotional secret during intimacy with your spouse and having them share it at lunch or in the locker room with friends the next day. Receiving the praise of others from the attention you'd draw to yourself is much like doing something to help someone in need and then telling everyone that you did it. God doesn't get the glory - you do! And you forfeit the reward He would have given because the attention, the praise and the accolades that you receive from people become your reward so God is no longer obligated to reward you.

During times of fasting there may be specific instructions given to you by God to give up specific things for a period of time rather than a complete fast of abstaining from all foods or desires. Again this is because fasting is personal and there may be certain things God is trying to get your attention about and this can sometimes be best done by you having to focus on one specific area of desire in your life. For me there are times when I have to give up my favorite drink in the whole world. Anyone who knows me can tell you it is a very popular cola product which I love to drink ice cold, right at the freezing point, but not frozen. I literally crave this soft drink yet there are times when the Lord will challenge me to give it up for stretches of time and, for me, this is extremely challenging since I barely miss a day without it.

FYI - anything that you love that much or say you cannot live without, will be challenged at some point in your walk with Christ. Not maybe. Definitely! When we become attached to things and people and we begin to esteem them too highly, they begin to establish themselves as idols or little gods in our lives. The Bible is more than clear on how God feels about this type of idol worship when He spoke the words "Thou shall have no other Gods before me." (EXODUS 20:3)

SEE ALSO EXODUS 20:3-6; 34:14; DEUT 4:24; 5:7-9.

The Lord says to us in His word that He will not share His glory with another. His glory is not just the outcome of His works and the praise for His accomplishments, but God's greatest glory is you, His prized creation. He will not share you with another. He is gracious and He gives us to each other as we live here on Earth and allows us the time and space we need for the people and responsibilities He's blessed us to have in our lives. All He asks, is that we make time for Him during our day, everyday, and that we consecrate specified blocks of time periodically just for Him. We have the rest of our days, weeks, months, years and lives to honor our spouse, our children, our jobs, our desires, and each other. Don't you think He deserves just a portion of that?

I say to all who are serious about growing, disciplining and purging their lives, bodies and spirits with fasting, that if you can make up in your mind that there is nothing in the world as important as you getting what you need to get from God, your outcomes in every area of life - even with fasting - will be forever changed. What am I saying? I had those days when

I let the hunger pains get the best of me and convinced myself that God didn't want me to have the headache or the stomach cramps so I would break my fast and eat. As so many of us have - and some still do - I used the very familiar line of scripture "the spirit is willing but the flesh is weak" to my own advantage. The reality of it was that I gave in and I allowed my flesh to win over my spirit. Yes, the Lord knows we are human and that our flesh can be weak, however He doesn't allow for us to use that as an excuse when He is requiring dedicated time of us. This sentiment was spoken out of the mouth of Jesus to the disciples when He prayed in Gethsemane before He was arrested, tried and crucified. (SEE MATTHEW 26:36-40)

TAKE INVENTORY

What is it that you idolize? Is it your relationship? Is it your home, your cars? Is it money or your job? Maybe it is food, sex, your clothes, shopping? Could it be a cell phone, a TV program that you cannot miss an episode of? In order to really understand these things and how they rate in your priorities, you must - with honesty and pureness of heart - take inventory of your life and see what qualifies as a potential idol. It could be any of these things that I have mentioned previously or possibly something that I didn't mention. You would know what they are and where they fit in your life, simply by the desire you have for them. Now please understand, God wants you to have nice things and enjoy them, He wants us to be in loving relationships and really enjoy them, so these are not sins; however, it is important for you to realize that anything or anyone in our lives that we can neglect God for has the potential of becoming sinful to us. They can be detrimental - even deadly - to your relationship with Christ and must be overcome to obtain certain victories in your life. So you must always remember that the enemy is cunning and will use your body and your very human nature against you to keep you from reaching certain levels in your walk with Christ. But with a fervent prayer life for everyday things and fasting for the extra rough days, you can overcome these things.

PUT THEM TOGETHER!

By now you know that you can pray for many things and they will come to pass. You also know that in times of increased need or pressure that you can kick things up a notch and fast for answers or results. But there are many other things and many other places in God that can be reached only with fasting AND prayer together.

The Bible tells us in Matthew 17:21, *howbeit this kind goeth out but by prayer AND fasting*. In this passage of scripture, Jesus was speaking to the disciples after casting out a lunatic spirit from a young boy. The disciples were puzzled because they didn't understand why they could not just pray and cast the devil out of this boy as they had in times past in similar situations. They failed to realize that this situation was not the same as in times past, but this was a more formidable enemy, a stronger opponent which meant that the usual tactics or measures taken (prayer) would not be enough to conquer this enemy and others of its kind. So when questioning the Lord about this, His answer was prayer AND fasting.

Now, you should know that this recollection of Bible happenings represents itself to you, the believer, as both literal and figurative. It is literal because it shows you that just as in the disciples' time there are some demons in your time that prayer alone will not work to gain the victory over. You will have to fast AND pray.

It is figurative because in the breaking down of this passage of scripture, it is evident that the disciples had come across demons or imps in the past and had been able to cast them out but for some reason, this time they were not able to. This time it wasn't business as usual because this enemy was prepared for what they were bringing. FYI - when you defeat an enemy, the word goes out. When the word goes out of your victory, the details of how you won will be included in the re-telling of events. This is for the purpose of your enemies' preparation so that the next time you find yourself engaged in warfare your enemy will be prepared for you. So since you know that this is happening what you must do is be prepared for your enemy. In essence this is what Jesus told the disciples when He told them about fasting and praying together. It is something that will prepare you ahead of time for the hard battle you must fight.

Going on a fast at the moment they realized that the lunatic spirit was not coming out of that little boy would've done the disciples no good. However, if they'd already been in preparation and training for this encounter, if they'd already been fasting AND praying, the results of this story would've been dramatically different. This is the same thing that you must - and will - face in your walk with Christ. For you, these demons or imps represent troubles or challenges that are out of the ordinary. A hard thing, if you will. When you are faced with the hard thing in your life, it is necessary to strap down and take it on like a charging army with every secret weapon in your spiritual arsenal. You must have the attitude that something is going to die.

When you take on the hard things in life with the combination of fasting and praying the first thing that happens is you let God know, "I am willing to kill whatever is in me that would keep me from being victorious in order to kill this enemy." Preparation is key! The best way to prepare for these things is to teach your body and train it. Deny it! Growing up in my grandfather's church, there were two days a week that we were called to fast for at least half the day - but grandpa and grandma would fast until dinner time. Personally, this is excellent self-discipline and excellent flesh discipline. Collectively, it is a regulated time in which we, as a corporate body, would unite in prayer and fasting for each other's needs as well as the needs of the ministry. If one alone is a more powerful spiritual warrior from fasting and praying, can you imagine the whole body united and standing in agreement?

Taking this stand, the Lord knows you mean business and the next one informed of your determined state is your enemy. Whether you are fighting principalities in a spiritual battle, a battle with your own flesh or even one where other persons are involved, the Christ in you will stand up and whatever or whoever it is that opposes you will see that you came for war and something will die in this battle!

Endurance is next. The Bible tells us in Ecclesiastes 9:11 - *For the race is not given to the swift neither the battle to the strong.* It then goes on to tell us a couple of times in the New Testament that *if we endure until the end, we will be saved.* What an awesome thing to know that our victory has already been predestined before the foundation of the world! I know that sometimes it may look like you are going down for the last time but you must remember that your end has already been written. The Lord Himself penned the end of your story back on Calvary and Satan knows this. He does not have the authority to rewrite your story. He wants you to do it for him. He can only try and discourage you to the point that you will walk off of the road that you are supposed to take (the road God planned for you). He can't change your outcome but he can try and convince you to change your outcome. You need to rise up and let the God in you rise up and scatter your enemies. And having said that, since you know what the end is, you must start acting like you know what the end is. Hold your head up, stick your chest out and say, "I'm going on in the name of the Lord! He told me what the end is going to be and I'm going all the way so I can see it with my own eyes!" The old saints would say, "I'm gon' run on to see what the end is gon' be!" They spoke it because they had an assurance of what their end was no matter how bad things looked. They believed what the Word said of their end.

You need to take a cue from their faith. It's win-win! It's like having a spiritual trust fund set up and knowing that all you have to do is go through the process of the schooling, the testing, finish your courses and get your degree. Then all that has been held in trust will be released to you guaranteed! Paul spoke of this in II Timothy when he said:

I have fought a good fight, I have finished my course, and I have kept the faith. Henceforth there is laid up for me a crown of righteousness, which the Lord, the righteous judge shall give me at that day: (this is the part that includes you) AND NOT TO ME ONLY, BUT TO ALL THEM ALSO THAT LOVE HIS APPEARING. (2 TIM 4:7-8)

Endure until the end. Your reward is being held in trust - all you have to do is finish the course. This isn't something that might be waiting for you at the finish; it IS waiting for you at the finish! Set your face in the direction of the prize and don't stop until you get there. The only thing that remains now is for you to have the victory! Receive it!

Chapter Three
HIS WILL OR YOUR ANSWER?

You may have heard the saying "be careful what you wish for." I'd rephrase it and say, "be careful what you pray for." Why? Because you just might get it. For this reason it is important when you pray to ask God that His will be done in your life. Many times the things we ask God for are not in line with what He has planned for us, and at the end of the day, His way is always best because He sees not only what's in front of you, but He also knows what lies ahead of you that your eyes do not see.

On my album *Mirror, Mirror*, I had the opportunity to record a song called "I Know Who Holds Tomorrow". The lyrics of that song say "many things about tomorrow I don't seem to understand but I know who holds tomorrow and I know who holds my hand!" What a powerful statement! However those words are just the lyrics to another song unless you understand the depth of them. If I can never see past today, if I am deaf, dumb and blind and still have to walk into my future, I can walk with the assurance that potholes and oncoming traffic or any of the other elements I could encounter that can injure or kill me cannot harm me because I understand that the one who holds my tomorrow is the same one who holds my hand. Isn't that someone you'd want to be in communication with? Better yet isn't that someone you'd want to have direct access to at any time? Even more, what if you had a relationship with this someone? That's what prayer is. It is your unlimited direct access to commune and fellowship with God. When you pray there is nothing that can stop Him from hearing your request and if He hears you, He will answer.

That's not the end of the answer to prayer. I need you to understand the difference in receiving an answer from God and receiving the will of God as the answer.

We can pray and beg God for things that our flesh wants and not be in tune with what He is trying to show us for our lives. We pray and beg and cry and plead and God is yet trying to show you something better.

The scenario is much like that of a child (we'll call him Johnny) begging his parents for an ice cream cone and momma says no. Johnny says, "Mommy, I've been good. Why can't I have some ice cream?" and momma says, "It's too hot for ice cream, baby, it's going to melt and you'll get all messy." Johnny says, "Please daddy, please daddy, I've been a good boy!" Daddy says, "You don't need it right now, it will turn your stomach." Not wanting to take no for an answer Johnny begs more. "Please, mommy, you promised! Why can't I have it?" And momma says, "I know that looks good, but you can't have that kind of ice cream, its not good for you! Besides we are going out for sundaes at the ice cream parlor after dinner, just wait! You can't have a cone now and a sundae later." However, Johnny whines and starts saying, "You promised me I could have a treat and all I want is this ice cream cone! I don't care about the sundae! All of my friends are getting ice cream from the truck and I want to eat my ice cream with my friends now!" Finally mom and dad get tired of the whining and let Johnny have his way.

Now, before I make the connection, let me just tell you that Johnny would've never made it in my house! Moving right along…

Sometimes we pray and we tell the Lord, "Oh God I want this and I want that," and all He wants us to do is wait. He's not even saying no, just wait. But because we are so focused on what everyone else is doing; this one got a car and this one got married and that one just bought a house and everybody is moving along, we say, "Oh Lord, I don't want to be left behind and I'm dating this real nice guy right now and he visits church with me sometimes and he's got a good job and he says he wants to settle down and start a family, so why do I have to wait Lord?" After so much of Him trying to show you the benefit of patiently waiting, He allows you to have your way.

You get married - *Johnny gets his ice cream cone*. You buy a house - *it tastes so good*. You have a couple of babies - *Johnny got a double cone with the vanilla and chocolate swirl, yummy*. You had to stop working because of the children - *it is a little warm outside, just like mom said*. The raise your spouse was expecting didn't come and you can't go back to work yet - *Johnny's ice cream is starting to run down the cone*. It's getting increasingly difficult to make ends meet - Johnny's *racing to eat faster because the ice cream is now running down his arm*. You are arguing over every little thing now – *it's melting too fast for Johnny to keep eating*. Your marriage is a mess and you don't know how to fix it - *Johnny is a complete mess from what used to be a towering ice cream cone*. You are physically worn - *Johnny's stomach is upset from eating too fast trying to preserve the cone and keep his ice cream from melting and the mess getting everywhere*. You are hurting because your relationship is torn and you are faced with having to clean up and rest up before you can get up and start again - *Johnny had to throw the cone away, run to avoid getting stung by the bees, go home and wash up and then lay down for a while because while eating the ice cream, in effort to be included in the circle of friends, Johnny forgot that he was lactose intolerant!*

Now, I agree that this illustration is somewhat extra as far as the dramatics go, but it is relational, and we have all been where Johnny was for real. If Johnny had waited, instead of trying to keep up with the crowd, he could've sat in an ice cream parlor with his parents (his protectors) and had a sundae with all of the trimmings. Whipped cream, nuts, cherries, hot fudge, caramel – completely tailored to his specifics and made just for him and served in a bowl so that when the temperature from the atmosphere would begin to affect the firmness of the ice cream there would be no mess and minimal waste because even the melted part can be eaten if it's contained and not wasted. Not only that but Daddy would've made sure that instead of ice cream that the sundae would've been made with non-dairy frozen yogurt! BECAUSE DADDY KNOWS THAT JOHNNY IS LACTOSE INTOLERANT!!!

You feel me?

The same applies with the real life comparison. The marriage thing was looking good - not just because of loneliness, but because everyone else was doing it too. If only this lady could've waited just a little while longer, she could've received the equivalent to a royal banana split! Instead she got a cone that couldn't be preserved because it couldn't take the elements in the air.

The question here is what are you really after when you pray? Do you really want what's best, or do you want what's best looking for now? There comes a time where God will allow us to have our way, even if it's not His will. That is for all the immature Johnny's that cannot wait. What you get may be good in the beginning, but only God knows what lies ahead and around the corner where your eyes cannot see. Discipline yourself to learn how to be patient and wait for His will, rather than your answer. When you beg and cry and plead while praying and never stop to take the time to hear what He is saying back to you, chances are you are really more interested in getting your answer. The challenge of today is to willingly convert the type of prayer relationship you have with the Father and make it truly what it's supposed to be - an intimate conversation and communing between a Father and His child. Be more willing to wait and be patient even if it means your flesh has to die a little - which is usually what needs to happen anyway.

There are two outcomes for two very different types of prayer relationships. It is up to you to decide where you want to be. You will pray and God will give "your answer" or you will pray and His will answers. If you have been praying to God the way Johnny begged for that ice cream, take a minute now and ask God to forgive you. Tell Him you really want a relationship with Him and that you want to mature. You want to know what its like to have real intimacy in your conversation with Him. You want the outcome of your prayers not to be "your answers" but "His will answers."

Chapter Four
WATCH YOUR MOUTH!

Watch you mouth, watch your mouth what you say;
Watch your mouth, watch your mouth what you say;
For the Father up above is looking down in tender love,
Watch your mouth, watch your mouth what you say.

I learned this song in the primary class at Sunday school when I was no more than four years old. The message was clear and simple enough for a baby to understand it, yet sometimes adults don't get it. Maybe we should start singing this song to each other.

Words are powerful. You have heard your whole life the familiar chastisement "watch your mouth!" - especially when you were a child. That statement held much more truth and value than any of us could've imagined at that time. Now that you are older, that statement holds more weight than it did during your childhood and adolescent years, because as a mature and sensible adult, you realize that you can't just say whatever you feel like saying, even if you are provoked, because, with it now comes accountability. It was important then because it kept you from being chastised or punished by your parents or guardian. It is important now because it keeps you from being chastised or punished by God. It is imperative that we learn, as Christians growing in our faith, that we are accountable in the sight of the Lord for everything we do and say, whether good or bad.

HOW DO I LEARN TO WATCH MY MOUTH?

How do you learn to watch your mouth when for years and years - possibly your whole life - you have just spoken whatever comes to your mind? This is a challenge, but I would like to encourage those of you who know you have "mouth problems" by saying that no one is exempt from this learning process. Even for those who may not have a problem with speaking out of their emotions all the time, they too must "watch their mouths". We all hold casual conversations, which can sometimes result in things being said that shouldn't be said. As such, we are all guilty of speaking death to our life. For example, the wife of the unsaved husband can make the statement "he's never going to change." That statement - even after consecrating time and time again for her husband - can begin to undo the fruits and the benefits of her decreeing, fasting and praying. All this by allowing herself to speak the wrong thing because of a moment of disgust or anger. We must watch our mouths! So, again, how do we do this?

How do we watch our mouths? We must think before we speak. We must practice speaking positive, edifying, fruitful things over our lives and into our spirits as a matter of regular conversation and it will become habit. We must watch our mouths not to speak negative things over each other or ourselves, especially in anger. Think before you speak. How many times have you said something cruel to a person in the heat of the moment and then were sorry for it later? Know this. Words are life! Words are death! How many times can you recall using the familiar phrase "I take back what I said?" Sorry! You cannot take back what you say once it has been said. When you speak words, they are on a mission. Sent out to perform a task and - good or bad - those words are going to do what you sent them to do at that moment, even if you change your mind about what you said later on! The only thing that can stop the words that have already gone out of your mouth is a more powerful word sent behind it to counter and destroy it! If we really thought about that, we'd think twice - even a hundred times - before we say some things. WATCH YOUR MOUTH!

Remember this one? *"Sticks and stones may break my bones but names will never hurt me!"* Yes! The little nursery rhyme we learned as kids. And another one of the familiar phrases we grew accustomed to using. Cute, huh? CUTE AND WRONG!

Names can and will hurt you. A child who is constantly told they are dumb, ugly, and will never be anything doesn't stand a chance against a child who always hears how intelligent they are, how beautiful they are and that they can do or be anything they want in life. Your parents, grandparents and all the other old folk who used to hush you up and tell you to watch your mouth were uttering the wisdom of God into your life and you didn't even know it. But they did. They understood that they were imparting something to you that one day would save you from destruction.

We say that we understand that we have the authority and a covenant right to speak a word into our own lives to evoke change, but many of us really don't get it. If we did, our standard of living would be much higher. We wouldn't be crying the blues about needing money to pay bills all the time. We would have it. We wouldn't complain so much because rather than go over every possible negative for every situation we would ring out praises or begin to talk about resolution. We'd speak into our atmosphere and change the energy around us so that our mood would change. Once your mood changes, your outlook can change, and once your outlook changes, you can start making better decisions. You think more clearly. You can hear more clearly. You can see more clearly. That's really all you need.

Ask yourself, "When is the last time I exercised the power of speaking a word to turn things around in my life?" Have you ever done it? If not, I am here to serve notice that you are living beneath your privilege. The Bible couldn't make it clearer than when it said *speak those things that be not* (right now) *as though they were* (as if it's already done!). It is your covenant right!

Chapter Five
WORDS HAVE LIFE, WORDS ARE LIFE

THE FATHER'S EXAMPLE
This isn't something the Lord would have us do without an example for us to follow. No! This principle dates back to before there was an Earth. God used His words and spoke into nothing. It was literally black space from which God created an entire Universe. God led by example.

And the Earth was without form and void and darkness was upon the face of the deep..........
And God said let there be light and there was light
(GENESIS 1:2 PARTIAL, 3)

And God said, "*Let there be....*" God kept saying it until the job was complete! Earth, sky, bodies of water, sun, moon, stars, creatures of all kinds, plant life. He kept speaking until the Earth was full of life, movement, energy, vibrancy and color. God spoke it and it came to pass. This same ability He gives to you because He loves you and desires for you to be happy and fulfilled in life. No matter how bad things are, there is no void or emptiness too great that you cannot speak in to and cause change and abundance to come to it. God filled the spaces of galaxies and universes with the words of His mouth. Your empty and dark spaces, your places that are without form and void, by comparison, are closet space - at best, a room. How much talking is it really going to take to fill your closet or your room with color and energy and joy and success? God saw darkness and emptiness so He started talking. The more He spoke, the more things showed up. The more things showed up, the more He saw room for enhancement, so He kept talking. God spoke until every space in the Earth was filled. Everything that Earth would ever need to function and maintain itself was placed inside of it at the time of creation. Then God thought about us and said "Let us make man in our image." We were special to Him. So He already knew that this part of creation was going to take place a little differently. God didn't say *let there be man*, He said *let us make man*. He proceeded to, with His own hands, take the time to mold us from the Earth in His own image. The beauty in all of that is from the time we were conceptualized in the mind of God, we were already precious to Him. He wanted us to have an intimate and personal encounter with Him from the beginning so He shaped us from the Earth with His hands. And because the Earth already has everything in it that it will ever need for its own beauty, survival and replenishing, we, who were formed from the Earth, already have everything inside of us that we will ever need to function in life and live abundantly. Again - we are made of the Earth and the Earth was completed with everything already in it that it would need to maintain and produce for its survival and continuance. So with those ingredients, God molded us in His image, breathed His breath of life into us and empowered us to speak with the same authority to bring things into existence. What we need lingers inside of us because it's in the Earth and we are made of the Earth. We must only speak it out of our mouths and cause it to be. We must speak into our nothingness and cause something to appear. And in order to achieve that, you must first change the way you look at your circumstance. Begin to see the nothingness in your life not as nothingness or emptiness, but rather as a clean palette or an unpainted picture. Now see yourself as the artist and God has given you new art supplies saying, "Your mouth is the brush and your life is the canvas, now open your mouth and paint your destiny!" There is no dark void in your life that can out size the dark void that God had to fill to create the world. Your problems can never be that big. And if He could fill that much dark, empty space with just the words of His mouth, how much more can you fill your dark places by the words of YOUR mouth?

Of His own words God says this:

So shall my word be that goes forth out of my mouth: it shall not return unto me void, but it shall accomplish that which I please and it shall prosper in the thing whereto I sent it.
(ISAIAH 55:11)

The key is to line your will up with His. This is what happens. When you have submitted your will to God's will, your desires change. The things you want out of life begin to change. You begin to want for yourself what God wants for you - which is why He will not deny you because your will becomes His will. So when you speak things over your life, God then promises that whatsoever you bind on Earth, He Himself will bind in heaven and whatsoever you loose on earth He will loose in heaven.

So it works a little like this:

God speaks in eternity and drops into your spirit, "I want a bigger house in a better neighborhood."You think it and begin to desire it.You speak it and God speaks it back to you. The promise in Isaiah 55:11 begins to go to work. Your faith increases and blessings follow, then favor follows the blessings. You are looking at houses that you never thought you could afford to buy and before you know it, you are at the closing table. God honors your words because they were born of the desire that He put in you, making it His will for your life, binding Him in all of His power to come into agreement with what you pray for or decree (speak) over your life! It is the desire of the Father to give His children good gifts!

THE SON'S EXAMPLE
Then there was the revelation of Christ to the world as the Word.

In the beginning was the Word and the Word was with God and the Word was God.
JOHN 1:1

So important is the acknowledgment of the power of the Word that Jesus took it on as a name for which He wanted to be known. He didn't really need to take on any other names with all the ones that we already call Him: the Son of God, the Son of David, Emanuel, the Prince of Peace, Wonderful Counselor, Almighty God, etc. But so important it is to Him that you understand - He would give you permission to call Him the Word. So really, when you speak the Word, you speak Jesus! And when you give a word or decree, you do it by the authority of Jesus. So if your word is Jesus, done in the name of Jesus, with the authority of Jesus then I believe it's going to come to pass! This is why we must watch our mouths. For the privilege to attach Jesus and all the authority that goes along with Him to the words of our mouth, it now becomes your non-retractable, irrevocable responsibility to keep pure the instrument (your tongue) that would carry His name and the authority you've been given to use it at your disposal.

So we, the sons of God created in His image, and are heirs and joint heirs with Jesus Christ, possess the ability and the right to use the same authority He used when He spoke to unclean spirits and told them to leave and they went. We can do as He did when He commanded the lame to rise and walk and they got up. The Lord spoke a word and sent it to the home of the centurion so that his servant would be healed. He never set foot in the house, let alone laid hands on him. (MATTHEW 8:5-13)

God gave us power in our words because He knew that there would be times when our words would need to go where we couldn't. Why would you not want to take advantage of a gift like this when it is your blood-bought right? We need to discipline ourselves. Understand that we already do it everyday; we just don't apply it to great things. Instead we spend time complaining about what someone else has and what we don't have and why we don't like that person and how they make us sick! We waste words with nonsense!

Yes, the old people told us to watch our mouths; they also told us to think before we speak. Boy, if we had listened to half the stuff they told us, how much farther in life would we be? But we didn't listen because although we loved granny an' nem, they were old fashioned. "My professor said …" and "You know, I read a book about that same thing that said …" Let me give you some advice with your ultra-modern, super-educated, that-stuff-they-said-is-old-school thinking self. If you want to make it in this life, you sure better learn how to eat the meat and spit out the bones! It's definitely true that the old saints didn't have a lot of book knowledge, but what they didn't have by formal education; they gained by life experience and the wisdom of God.

Somebody must have needed that right there because that wasn't even a part of this chapter. Okay, back to thinking before you speak.

What would happen if you really thought before you spoke? If you can speak the word that you will have a good day today no matter what happens, why can't you speak the word that your body will come in line with the Word of God and function properly? Why can't you speak "peace be still" into your chaotic atmosphere and peace follows? It is all about what you believe. Then you can speak with power, conviction and authority and then watch the things you speak come to pass.

Chapter Six
THE POWER OF SPEAKING WORDS VS THE POWER OF SPEAKING A WORD

Death and Life are in the power of the tongue:
And they that love it shall eat the fruit thereof.
PROVERBS 18:21 KJV

In everyday language this means: the tongue is powerful. It's powerful enough to cause death and powerful enough to cause life - covering all things in between. Those that love the power that they have will pursue it and live off of everything that that power will provide for them while they are alive.

Nowhere in that scripture does it say to the born-again believer do I give the power of life and death in the tongue. Nope. Sorry this is common among man and in the mind of a corrupt person with great focus, this is a dangerous weapon. The news is anyone can speak words and they manifest. The good news is that only a child of God can speak a word to overtake any other words spoken.

Yes, it's true! A God-empowered word can overtake words spoken by just another sharp-tongued person who seeks to misuse and manipulate for his own purpose the gift of power through words that God gave every man. So every tongue does have power, but a cleansed tongue, a sanctified tongue, has immeasurable power because the possessor of it has the favor and backing of God Almighty to assure that what he or she speaks will surely come to pass. Even if words have been spoken against what you have spoken.

As I have mentioned before, the ability to speak a thing and it come to pass is not something that is exclusive to the believer, but rather a common gift given to all humankind, just like free will. This is why there are some people who always seem like no matter what goes on in their life, they can bounce back. I think we all can look in our lives at some point and find a person like that. If you take a closer look at that person and to the things that they do and say, you will find that these are the same who carry the attitude that failure is not an option. They speak success to themselves, they work to make it happen and, as a result, they always walk across success. There is an old saying that you should always reach for the moon, so even if you fall short, you'll land among the stars. This is what keeps those individuals always at the height of what they do. It is my firm belief that no one should live better than the children of God. And for all of you who counter with "we are all the children of God," I'm talking about the children who are in relationship with their Father. Your relationship with the Father is what makes the difference between the words that come out of your mouth and the words that come out of the mouth of the unbeliever. They can speak words about things and they will come to pass whether they are good or bad but your relationship with the Lord causes the things that you say to come with His endorsement, empowering and fueling the words that you speak. This enables your words to counter and make void a word that may have the wrong intention behind it. Thus the difference in speaking words and speaking a word.

Speaking words over something or someone is powerful but carnal, crafty, soulish and selfish. Speaking a word over something or someone is Godly, prophetic, spiritual and selfless. Which would you rather do?

There are dominant characteristics associated with the power of the tongue and speaking words vs. speaking a word. Because of the very opposite natures of these very similar operations it is important that you have an understanding of what they are.

THE GOOD

The power or ability to speak life rests in your mouth. That power was given to man as a great gift, but it is also a huge responsibility. You have the authority and the ability to speak change into negative circumstances. You can stop the plan of the enemy with what's in your mouth! You have the power to speak over a negative word that has already been spoken and kill it before it manifests itself. The problem is that we really don't believe we can do this. Another great problem is that we are simply too casual in our conversation. We don't take thought before we speak. This has proven to be a great victory tool for the enemy of our soul because he doesn't even have to work on keeping our blessings from us in this respect. Some of us don't believe we deserve it and others just don't believe! Whichever is the case, you make the devil's job that much easier. The doubt and unbelief that we allow to take residence in us, does all the work for him. Many times it is easier to get unsaved people to believe that they can speak positive change into their lives than it is to get the Christian to believe it and act on it. You are who I would call the unbelieving believer. More commonly known as Doubting Thomas, you have your finger in Jesus' wounds and still don't believe it's Him. You who have witnessed miracles and blessings. You who have felt the presence of God and know what it is to be transformed by His power, you who carry this gospel from place to place and person to person, yet are missing out on something that was meant for our enjoyment and pleasure as the children of God. You won't speak good things into your own lives because you don't believe. Of course, you say you do, but let's keep it real - if you really did, you would walk around everyday finding some wonderful new thing to speak into your life and you would be enjoying the taste of the fruit of your lips! But alas, you don't believe so you don't bother. It's almost as if we want to suffer! It's like being given the cure for a deadly disease and knowing that you have the disease but you won't take the cure. It's time to wake up and know who you are, *whose* you are and what that entitles you to. Speak it everyday! "I am the righteousness of God, I am the head and not the tail, I am above and not beneath, I am healthy and strong, I am healed, I will live and not die and declare the works of the Lord! I am blessed, I am happy, and I do have joy! All of my bills are paid and I am walking in prosperity! My family members are saved, my business is prosperous, my marriage is strong and my kids are healthy and wise!" Believe it! Practice it! Preach it! Teach it! Not to the masses but to yourself and to your household! It starts at home. Repeat it with your spouse! Chant it with your children. Make up a song about it, but whatever you do - JUST DO IT!

THE BAD

Where there is good there is bad. Your mouth is no exception to that rule. For all the good things that can happen as a result of you practicing the power of speaking a word, there are as many negative things that can happen when you just speak words. The tongue is a heavyweight and can take a person out if used the wrong way. It is a weapon and it injures and cuts down to the soul if used effectively with improper motives. Words can kill. They always affect who we are and what we become. That is why it is so important to speak the right things over your life. Again, I have to reiterate that, as Christians, we have allowed ourselves to be so common that we have become desensitized to the very power that lies and works in us everyday. Thereby making the Devil's job to rob of us who we are, what we are called to be and what we are meant to have, very easy.

Yes, the power in the tongue is a gift. The rule generally is that gifts given that go unused will find themselves dormant inside of the believer. Not in this case. It is important that you understand if you are not using your gift of power in the tongue with Godly intent and purpose, it is being used another way whether you mean for it to or not. So I would urge you to pay attention and give your words intention under the authority of Jesus Christ. Beware of the everyday pitfalls in conversation. Common catch phrases to look for are "I can't", "I'm not", "I don't have", "I can't afford", "I'll never" and any other phrase that leads to you speaking negatively over yourself or someone else.

We all have been affected by words spoken over our lives at some point and we live those words out everyday. Good or bad, we are the living words of someone before us. We live, work and worship with people who are victimized and trapped in a life painted by the brush of someone else's mouth. We say that there is nothing to it or it's just that people need to get over the past and move on. But you must remember, anytime words go un-countered, they will manifest and must be lived out until such a time comes that "a word" can be spoken to undo what was already done by the soulish words spoken originally.

Just think of the child who never heard anything good about himself while growing up. He does grow up but he becomes an adult with little or no self-esteem. These are they who walk around us daily with a little, insecure and bruised child hidden in their innermost parts. They can be the most brilliant business minds, the most athletic, the most talented or the greatest intellects, but that hidden part of them remains lurking in the shadows of their souls with the cruelty and the stigma that haunts them from the terrible things that were said to them as children. They can move around in society and function to great degrees of normalcy, even excellence, yet seeking the approval of people to fulfill their void of self worth. They grow up with great social defenses in place - whether it's fighting physically or strong senses of cynicism or sarcasm using words themselves to hurt people. These are the no-nonsense, I'm-not-having-it people you see everyday at work and church and in the neighborhood. They seem so strong, but somehow they almost always end up looking for love in the wrong places. They adorn themselves with church and community activities, they perfume themselves with the scent of the social butterfly, but somewhere along the way, the stench of emotional sores that have been festering within begins to rise. It usually shows up in the relationships they have with their own children. Though the abused child will often grow up saying, "I will never treat my children that way," - if they go unhealed, they will find themselves cutting down the very souls of their own children and inflicting the same scars with their words. They will find themselves imprisoned in the vicious cycle of the mental and emotional abusers of their past and of the past of their mother or father and of their grandmother or grandfather and of their great grandmother or great grandfather and so on and so on and so on! We see these people everyday and we ignore their need for deliverance or we just convince ourselves that they are miserable human beings and we stay away from them. And it all started with some words.

Now think of this same child and if he was raised being told he was beautiful and smart and unstoppable. What if he had been told that he was loved and that life was better because he was born and helped to fulfill it. What if, from a young age, it had been embedded in his mind and spirit that he was destined for greatness, that God loved him and He placed him here on Earth for a great purpose? Without a doubt, that child would succeed in life at pretty much anything. Not because he is good at everything he goes after, but because he believes he is good enough for ANYTHING he goes after. Why? Because my daddy told me so! Because my mother told me so! Why won't little Sally let Johnny play under her skirt? Because her daddy told her that she is a jewel worth waiting for until marriage and if Johnny can't wait then he's not good enough for her! Even when Johnny tries to conquer little Sally with the three-word trump card - I LOVE YOU - Sally's daddy tells her that everyday and he told her Johnny would say that! Sally knows she is God's gift and she is! And it all started with some words.

We see this person all the time, too. But rather than celebrating them, what happens? We talk about them. We say, "She is so stuck up! He thinks he's better than everyone else because he grew up in that neighborhood." We are so used to seeing the ugly, that when beauty presents itself we trash it. WE MUST DO BETTER!

That's not the end of it.

What about the battered and emotionally abused woman? Beating after hellacious beating can take place, but long after the scars from the beatings have healed, the images and the words live on in her spirit and in her psyche. Healing is needed from the hateful words spoken to her throughout her life and that echo through her mind … you're ugly … you're fat … you're stupid … you're worthless … if you leave me where you gonna go? … No one will ever want you! Like a CD player programmed to repeat the same song. It never misses a beat and it comes in at the same place every time. It never gets silenced or turned off. The volume only goes down as time passes and other things begin to occupy the time and life of that woman. But right on cue, when the time comes and the opportunity for love and relationship introduces itself, the volume begins to slowly rise inside of her, often resulting in her not recognizing the real thing when it finds her. She will fight it, because introducing healthy love to a battered and emotionally abused woman is the equivalent of introducing a germ into a healthy body. It is considered an invader because it is unrecognized and the body begins to look for ways to force the germ to exit. An abused woman in a relationship with a loving and nurturing man will find a way - even unknowingly - to sabotage her own relationship because it is foreign to her and she feels like she is unworthy. She will often wander until she finds her way back into the arms of another abuser. Why? Because the words are always there playing in the background. It is the score* of her life and it will never go away without some learned coping skills that can be obtained through counseling coupled with the divine healing touch of Jesus Christ who has the power to make old things pass away and all things become new.

Now, I know I just messed with somebody's theology and possibly lost half of you deep and sanctified folk whose mantra is "as long as I got King Jesus I don't need nobody else!" Many of you still think psychology, therapy and counseling is an unnecessary tool of wellness for the saints, as long as we've got Jesus and the altar we don't need counselors. I will take the time to address that in full detail in another chapter.

*Score-*music usually written specifically for a movie and strategically placed at different places throughout to enhance the visual affect or the emotion of that moment where it was placed.*

Chapter Seven
THE WORDS OF MY MOUTH

Let the words of my mouth, and the meditation of my heart, be acceptable in thy sight, oh Lord, my strength, and my redeemer.
PSALM 19:14

I have been quoting this passage of scripture for almost as long as I have been alive. This Bible verse, thanks to my grandfather who used it as the benediction for every service in his church and still does, became one of the first scriptures I committed to memory. That scripture - along with "Jesus wept" and "remember the Sabbath day to keep it holy" – were my after-the-dinner-blessing scriptures. It was something I learned and knew only because I heard it almost everyday of the week. For many years that's all it was. It was my indicator that service was really over (since standing up for the benediction didn't necessarily mean we were going to be let out of service right then - especially if someone started talking and got things fired up again, all my Pentecostal babies can relate!) It was merely something I recited when it was time to leave service.

As I got older and I began to really pay attention to the words that I was saying, I began to understand that those are not just words, but the careful utterances of one who - with all sincerity - wanted never to offend God by speaking the wrong thing to Him or to anyone or even over his own life for fear that it would be displeasing to God whom he loved so much. This kind of revelation can only come to one from God. David understood that language and communication was a precious and powerful gift given to man by God and it was to be respected and used wisely at all times. I guess that's why David went on to say *I will bless the Lord at all times and His Praise shall continually be in my mouth*!

How different of a person would you be if you had the attitude of David in Psalm 19:14 and actually lived it out?

This subject is something that I don't feel is dealt with often enough with the body of Christ but it is something that is of great concern to God. We move about through our days and we talk about anything, just because we can. We talk about the weather. We talk about our health. We talk about our marriages. We talk about our kids. We talk about the church, the deacons, the ushers and the Pastor. We talk about each other. We talk ourselves right into a funk sometimes.

You know you've done it. You can be enjoying a good day and allow yourself to get sucked into conversation with the wrong person and end up in the nastiest mood for the rest of the day. Your conversation or words had the power to trigger an image or memory that triggered an emotion that changed the course of your day. Now you're mad or depressed, you can't concentrate on work or anything else, you're taking it out on your co-workers and family members, and God help the person driving in front of you! And it all got started with some words. Don't tell me words are meaningless.

The Bible tells us that the words of a man's mouth are as deep waters (Proverbs 18:4). Revelations such as this one should be good news to us, however because we are too often unwise with the use of our words, passages of scriptures would more often be used as a warning. I perceive then if you are not careful, you can inundate yourself with your own negative words or can be inundated by the negative words of another directed toward you, and if you are not careful, you can be drowned in a sea of negativity that was poured on by some words!

Let the words of my mouth and the meditation of my heart be acceptable in thy sight oh Lord my strength and my redeemer. Amen

WHAT IF I DON'T KNOW HOW TO PRAY?

Everyone knows how to pray but too often we have preconceived notions and get methods and religious regiments fixated in our heads and we believe that if we cannot meet a certain standard in our vocabulary, we cannot pray. Well, let me tell you that you are not the first to think that way and you certainly won't be the last.

Did you know that the disciples didn't know how to pray? Or rather, they convinced themselves that they didn't know how to pray, just like many of you. They walked everyday with Jesus and didn't know how to pray so they asked Him, *Lord teach us to pray* (Luke 11:1) *and he taught them what we now know as "The Lord's Prayer"* (Luke 11:2-4). This is usually the first prayer we learn to say as a child. That one or the children's grace prayer we had to say before eating a meal (God is great, God is good …). The Lord's Prayer is the ultimate guideline of what prayer should be like - it was honest, simple and to the point. There were no long, multi-syllabled words in use that would need to be translated. But in the same fashion in which He taught the multitudes in a manner that would be understood by all, not just in the days that He walked the Earth, but also until the end of time. In a few short lines, Jesus taught His disciples to speak words to the Father that honored Him, asked for forgiveness for themselves and grace to forgive others, sought provisions, as well as guidance to not be bound by the temptations we'd already been delivered from.

Prayer is sometimes viewed as a formal task that requires great knowledge of religion or the ability to use large words. So many of us back down from it, fearing that we will not say the right thing. There are no combinations of words that would make one prayer more powerful than another. There is only the sincerity of your heart. So even if you were to speak great words that reflect superior knowledge or intelligence, if the utterances are not in synch with the content of a pure heart, the prayer isn't even acceptable. In fact, it is a waste of time and you can rest assured that it went unnoticed and unheard in the Heavens.

The truth is that none of those big words and other formalities even matter. God wants us to communicate with Him and prayer is the vehicle He provided us with in order to do it. There is no situation too small or too large. He doesn't need you to tell Him about your circumstance. He's God, He already knows your afflictions, but the fact that you'd take the time to talk to Him says one thing, "I TRUST YOU LORD, and talking to You about the things that concern me makes me feel better." That's all He wants. He wants you to be the apple of His eye and He wants you to want to be the apple of His eye. So there really is no "way" to pray. Just talk to Him. It is understandable that the thought of talking to the one true Creator of the world and giver of life can be a little overwhelming.

It's also understandable when you think of Him that way, you should want for every little thing to be just right, but that would be a burden to you. However, that burden is lifted with the knowledge that because He is the Creator of the world and the giver of life that you don't have to be perfect when you come to Him. He already knows everything about you. Every mistake you've made. Even the one's you haven't made yet! God knows the secret things that no one knows. So when we come to Him, we are already naked. We don't have to front for God. And because He already knows everything, you can talk to Him about ANYTHING - NO SHAME!

PRIVILEGES OF PRAYER

There is a popular credit card company whose motto is "membership has its privileges." The privileges that go along with carrying this card have been known to make doing day-to-day business a little easier. When you pray and establish a relationship with the Lord, there are perks and bonuses that go along with it as well. How much easier could life be overall with the privileges that go along with a strong, healthy, well-established prayer life? Let's explore it.

1. **Calling those things which are not as though they were**
   There is no great mystery to this one. It means just what it says. Because of your established relationship with Him through prayer,

God will grant you the right to speak things into your life or into the life of others that do not already exist! How different would your life be at this very moment if you had the ability to change things just from the words you spoke?

2. **Prayer can stop the workings of your enemies**
   Yes, this is true. Through prayer, God will empower you to speak a word to your enemies and stop their plan of destruction for you. Also when you are in true relationship with the Lord, He will hear your cries to Him and be compelled to move mountains to ensure that His precious one is safe.

3. **Prayer will open up your understanding**
   Through prayer, God can really begin to give you wisdom to know and understand the word of God, which is your overcomer's manual for life. It will open your eyes to things that go on around you, both naturally and spiritually, and not just the major things, but also the things we deem insignificant. This new foresight and insight will enable you to make wiser choices in life overall and keep you from pitfalls that you may have otherwise fallen into.

4. **Prayer will give you perfect peace.**
   God promises to keep you in perfect peace if you keep your mind stayed on Him (Isaiah 26:3). Perfect peace. Most of us cannot even imagine what that is like. That would be everything going wrong around you and the world as you know it in an uproar, yet you can still sleep at night without taking pills. You can still eat and hold your food down without the Alka Seltzer. No headaches or worries because you have a covenant relationship based on prayer with the one who controls the outcome of it all. What an assurance! WHAT AN INSURANCE! But this insurance only comes with true relationship with the Father. The kind that can only be established through communing with Him and

sharing intimate times with Him in prayer.

5. **You always have back up!**
    When your enemies wage war against you, they are in for a real fight - one that may not require you to engage in battle. The Lord of Host our God who does fight for us will gladly let you rest while He handles your enemies. This is both natural and spiritual. The Bible is very clear on how God feels about anyone coming against His children. Entire nations have been wiped out as a result. Scripture tells us that it is a better fate for a millstone to be hanged around a person's neck and that they are tossed into the sea and drowned than to oppose the children of the Most High. It's like the kid who goes to school and has a big brother or big sister or, even better, several big brothers and sisters who go to school with him. He can walk around the school completely unintimidated because he knows he is protected. No one is going to bother with any of the children from that family because no one wants to have to deal with all of the siblings in that family. That's what this privilege is about - you being a member of a family that stretches around the world and into the Heavens. It's about knowing that your enemy knows if he messes with you, he messes with your whole family! Just like the movie. I think I like those odds.

Practice telling the enemy, go ahead:

SATAN, YOU MESS WITH ME, YOU MESS WITH MY WHOLE FAMILY!

SECTION II
Faith: You've Got It!

Chapter Eight

DIVINE HEALING OR DOCTOR'S HEALING?

I promised to get back to this subject for all of you who were interested in knowing where I stand on the matter of faith healing vs. physician healing.

PRAYER VS. PHYSICIAN, ALTAR VS. APOTHECARY, DOCTOR'S INSTRUCTIONS VS. DIVINE INTERVENTION

I sincerely thank God for you who trust so much in the power of prayer. It is that foundation that started me and so many others in our walk with Christ. The unrelenting belief that as long as we have the altar we don't need doctors is held more dominantly in number by our senior saints whom we love dearly. We don't criticize that, but rather celebrate it. We understand that when many of our senior saints were coming along the thought of a medical plan was unheard of. They didn't run to the doctor for every little pain like many people do today. In fact, most of the time they didn't go at all. In the instance that they got very sick and went, they would go and get diagnosed and if they couldn't afford the treatment or medicine they did exactly what the Word said.

Is any sick among you? Let him call for the elders of the church; and let them pray over him anointing him with oil in the name of the Lord:
And the prayer of faith shall save the sick, and the Lord shall raise him up; and if he has committed sins they shall be forgiven him.
JAMES 5:14, 15

This die-hard faith was born of real belief in the healing power of Jesus Christ and maintained mostly by extreme poverty and difficult circumstances. Many times their reality was that of, "if the Lord does not heal me then I am going to die." Even now in many countries around the world where extreme poverty is the rule and not the exception, people will walk for miles and journey for days when they hear of a man or woman of God who can heal them because they are desperate for a miracle. It's no wonder that our brothers and sisters in other parts of the world and even our grandparents and great grandparents who lived right here - saw more miracles than we do now. They lived for a move of God and their faith was unshakable. Their faith IS unshakable, simply by reason of what they lived. I believe that, in both instances, whether it is the senior saints or the impoverished Christian in this country or abroad who cannot afford a doctor, this type of faith qualifies them for miracles when no one else can seem to get one. For this reason, I have personally taken the scripture to another level that tells us to call for the elders of the church if there are sick among us. I believe that not only are the elders (ministers) qualified to call down healing from Heaven but I sincerely believe that the elder saints, by virtue of their faith in the healing power of God, can get quick results when they pray for these things. To some, these seem a little extreme because they won't put their trust in doctors at all. The only doctor many of them have ever known is Doctor Jesus. So they choose to stick with what has worked for their entire lives. You've heard it said before - IF IT AIN'T BROKE, DON'T FIX IT!

I applaud anyone who can stand so strong in his faith that way, however I also believe that is a personal choice of how to live. I strongly feel that those who believe that way cannot and should not belittle the faith of those who trust in medicine's ability to help heal their bodies when they are sick. Doctors are a gift from God to mankind and they are Biblical. I'll get back to that in a minute.

Now, how about the flip-side of that coin? What about those of you who can't get a paper cut without calling an ambulance, the HAZMAT unit, the fire department, the CDC and the American Red Cross? For every little thing, you need a prescription. Every time somebody asks you how you are feeling you're complaining about something and talking about your next doctor's appointment. There are some people that are addicted to going to the doctor! And don't let them have good insurance! Forget it. They're going to see specialists for body parts they didn't even know they had. Their medicine cabinets look like the overflow of the pharmacy's supply closet. And faith? Of course they have faith. They have faith in their HMO!

What is called for in this instance, just as in any other area of life, is the need for balance. A doctor's diagnosis and subsequent plan to achieve healing or wellness for their patient is just that - a plan. The believer has the edge on the non-believer when seeing the doctor because you have the power to speak life into the plan of the doctor and tell the Father to get in the plan, get in the medication, move through the hands of the surgeon and do something supernatural on your behalf. Your chances for total healing outweigh the chances of the non-believers by leaps and bounds because the spirit of healing goes before you by the stripes Jesus' received while being beaten nearly to death, so that the day you walked in your doctor's office to get those results thousands of years later, the plan for your healing was already in place. BY HIS STRIPES YOU WERE HEALED! IT WAS ALREADY DONE.

So it is a partnership. The Lord gave us doctors not to do away with divine healing, but to make divine healing easier to receive. The reality is that all healing - with or without the aid of a doctor - is divine. We are too finite minded to understand the mind and total will of God for our wholeness, both naturally and spiritually, so He simplifies Himself so we can understand the things He is trying to impart to us. Medical discoveries haven't been made because man was so smart. God supernaturally empowered the minds of these chosen vessels to bring out of the Earth what has been in it from the beginning of time. They gave it a name, bottled it and sold it and we call it medicine. It is the most brilliant marketing strategy of all time and eternity. Its God's healing in a form that you can understand, receive and most importantly, make sense of because it comes from the hand of a familiar face. And He did all of that to make you and I more comfortable.

The same goes for those Christians who feel that we shouldn't go to psychologists for treatment of emotional and mental issues. For so long this issue has been taboo among large groups of Christian society. Even many who don't take issue with receiving treatment from medical doctors for physical ailments, often have a problem with a psychologist treating the believer.

Allow me to respectfully say that if the discomfort in your spirit is with the saints putting the secrets of their souls in the open with a non-believer, then let us admonish one another to find someone to counsel that is both spirit-filled and qualified to counsel by credentials and by way of their education. But DO NOT CONDEMN THEM FOR SEEKING PROFESSIONAL HELP!

For those who do not have an issue with counseling by any qualified, educated therapist (Christian or not), I say get it! And then make your way to the altar for prayer and a good old-fashioned deliverance! Either way I believe that for many, both therapy and prayer are necessary for healing and closure.

This is my last point with the counseling and then I am going to move on to avoid sounding like the poster child for Psychology Today. For too long now we have dealt with emotional issues at the church and have not achieved total wholeness as a result. Although we've done our best to deal with these issues, professional help was never a consideration and somehow those issues never get fully resolved. Mainly because there are a lot of people in the church trying to administer healing for things they have never experienced total healing and deliverance from themselves. What happens is we have hurt touching hurt and rather than transferring healing, we teach others how to "deal" with life after the tragedy rather than how to overcome and live. As a result, we send out an army of wounded soldiers who - as long as they stay on a spiritual high - do okay and are feeling no pain. But as soon as they begin to come down, reality sets in and they are going home just as miserable as they were before they came to the altar for help. This becomes a cycle that gets repeated over and over again, Sunday service after Sunday service and Bible study after Bible study. And rather than the church being a place of healing, it becomes a place of medicating and good feeling. They come and it's a party. They feel good, they get high and we all go home. They come down (some faster than others), go back into the depression and start looking for the next high so they scope out revivals and crusades coming through town and look for the next prophet coming to the church down the street to tide them over until the next service at their own church. But through it all - no healing.

We have to stop this. There are so many emotional issues in the church and they must be dealt with. It's killing the Body of Christ. Rather than look down on the one who would seek counseling in addition to spiritual restoration for their healings, we need to encourage them. It has nothing to do with faith. God gave us these men and women with these superior learning capacities and understanding to help us. God uses them as His instruments of healing, and when healing takes place, God still gets the glory! When a person has cancer or some other major illness we don't advise them not to go to the doctor. We don't tell them they are less saved than the next Christian because they take chemotherapy. NO! They take the chemo and we pray that God would restore their body to wholeness. Therapy for emotional healing is the exact same thing.

I am going to sum this up with the wise words of my former pastor, "Ya'll need to go to the doctor, how else are you going to know what God healed you from when He heals you?"

JESUS' DOCTOR

I believe that was on Jesus' mind when He recruited Luke as a disciple. Luke was a doctor before he went on the road with Jesus and becoming a disciple didn't strip him of his qualifications or education. I believe Luke was able to bring the type of validation and proof to unbelieving spectators who might try to discredit the authenticity of the healings taking place during this movement that was going on when Jesus was evangelizing. Why else would He take a doctor? Jesus' mission was to save and to heal and to deliver so if He knew that's what He'd be doing, why would He bring a doctor with Him to the revivals and crusades? Do you think Luke was out there writing prescriptions and passing out Tylenol to the sick while Jesus was preaching? I don't think so.

I believe in my heart that Jesus always had in mind that the physician would be the extended hand of the healing ministry. That through doctors, the masses would be healed by something tangible and someone relational to their situation. God called doctors not to overtake or negate the works that He would perform, but to compliment and showcase the mighty hand of God. How many times have you heard of the doctor giving up on a patient only to say that it would take a miracle to save that person? When the miracle happens, even the most scientific-minded, non-miracle-believing doctor has to admit that there is something more at work. God placed a system in the Earth that brings light to the wonderful healer that He is and we shouldn't fight it. The saints need to have a doctor's report when they are testifying to the world that "the doctor said I was going to die, but I went to the Father and He did what the doctor couldn't do." The testimony becomes a witness tool, even to the doctor who would know better than anyone else how much of a walking miracle you are! Jesus' light shines to the physician through you and the physician becomes the ad agency for the miraculous work of our God. WHAT A SETUP!

So exactly where do I stand on the issue of divine healing vs. doctor's healing? For the one who is ailing physically, to you I say that there is nothing that compares to the healing power of Jesus Christ. For He was wounded for our transgressions, bruised for our iniquities, the chastisement of our peace was upon Him and with His stripes, we were - and are - healed. For those who have been through emotionally and mentally destructive times, to you I say trust in the Lord your God who gives the peace that surpasses all of man's understanding and puts broken hearts back together. For some of you there will be miraculous healings, and for others, your miracle will come through the anointed hands of a man or woman who God has empowered to heal through the practice of medicine. For those who do not receive an act of divine healing, I say go to the doctor - all while you are following these Biblical guidelines and reminding your mind, body and spirit who their Creator is and why they must come subject to God's plan for your healing even through the medication. These two extremes of healing were made to work together and compliment and aid each other for a purpose. Whether your healing comes through a prescription or through prayer, in the end it is your faith combined with God's ultimate will for your life that brings the results.

Chapter Nine
THE FEAR FACTOR

There is a television show of the same name that my children love to watch. It comes on once a week and is comprised of stunts or assignments that are all designed with bringing your worst fears to the surface. They usually involve speed, heights, water and something absolutely disgusting to eat. There are several contestants and a host whose sole purpose is to introduce you to the object of fear and try to convince you either to walk away before you ever try to overcome it, or taunt you the entire time to get you to quit before you complete the assignment. Sometimes there are bonuses and gifts given along the way as incentive to encourage the completion of certain assignments or stunts, but there is a large monetary prize given in the end for the one contestant who overcomes their fears and completes each task.

Now, I watch this show with my kids every week (and every week they look forward to making fun of me because without fail they know that I am going to be grossed-out by the eating stunt), and the one thing I have gathered, from watching the show unfold every week, is that in order to make it through any or all of the assignments that are given, there has to be a determination to win and conditioning of the mind. I have also gathered that having one without the other is no good and will ultimately work against the contestant. Yes, it is true that physical strength and velocity are assets to make it through many of the stunts successfully, however the ability to bench press 350 pounds will not help you when the host tells you to eat a bowl of live bugs while sipping on spoiled milk. That requires conditioning of the mind to overcome what you see so you can get past it and move on to the next thing. So in the end, the one contestant prepared to face their fears and endure until the end, no matter what happens, will be the one who walks away with the prize.

So what does all of that have to do with you? Your journey through life and your walk with Christ are all knitted together as one long trip, from conception to death. Time and time again each one of us can look back over our lives and see things that we have missed out on because we were too afraid to go after it. We know it and we live with the haunting thoughts of "what if I had just?" "What if I went?" or "I wonder…" and then to pacify ourselves we will sing the old familiar song "well, it never would've happened anyway" and we move on until the next time something triggers those thoughts. Have you ever wondered why you can see someone who reminds you of yourself (or someone who reminds you of your former self), and get very excited about their energy, ability and drive to succeed? You get so excited about them that you almost lose yourself in what they are doing - as if it was you, your dream, and your hope. That is called a stirring. Do you even know why this happens? This happens because the things that God put in you to live life abundantly and successfully remain in you although you haven't done anything with it. They lie dormant in you like a sleeping giant waiting to be awakened so it can conquer! The thing that lives in that person around you is kindred to what sleeps in you and it connects. The energy and the excitement that you feel as a result of being around that person is because what God put in you is still alive and can be rejuvenated! That feeling of life that comes over you is not for you to tell yourself that used to be me and it is too late. God allows you to feel that because He wants you to know that it's not too late. Death is the end. If the chance of your success in life and with the gifts God put in you were over, you wouldn't - couldn't - feel anything. Guess what? You are not dead! You are reading this book, which means you are alive and all that is within you has a chance at being revived.

BUT FIRST YOU MUST LET GO OF FEAR! And I am going to help you do that.

FEARLESS FAITH OR FAITHFUL FEAR?

We all have faith, or what I believe is the beginning of faith, that God put in each of us. I call it the inner expectation mechanism. Whether we walk in faith or in fear we all start out at that common position. The name it will have is based on how we groom and cultivate it with thoughts, words and deeds. Even the one that can't seem to trust God for anything possesses it.

There are two kinds of faith and no matter who you are, you walk in one or the other. There is the Un-faith Faith, or *fear* as it's more commonly known, and then there is the God Kind of Faith - wholly trusting, leaning and depending on His Word and ability. Those who have the latter are the ones who speak great testimonies of overcoming impossible situations, even before they happen. As a result, great healings, miracles, blessings and deliverances follow them wherever they go because they cling to the promises of Jesus like a chronic asthma patient clings to his/her pump! It's their lifeline, and everything they do is based on the faith they have in their Savior. They walk it, they talk it, they live it, they breathe it, they act on it and they don't make a move without it. They understand that it is the thing that will take them from glory to glory.

You say you've tried and no matter how hard you try, you just can't seem to muster up that kind of faith because it's just too hard. I am going to show you just how capable you are of living in the realm of faith. In fact, I'm going to show you that in the state you are presently in, you are full of faith and have simply misused it. Once you realize just how full of faith you are and that life could've been very different for you by now, you may not be very pleased with yourself, but this isn't designed to bring you into condemnation concerning your walk. This is only to show you what you have always had inside of you, what you can do with what you have and bring correction to your situation so you can move on and live in victory.

Let's use for example: You have a child that you have been struggling with. You raised this child with values and morals and to love and fear the Lord - or maybe you didn't. Whatever the circumstances, God made you a promise concerning this child. He told you that this child would live and not die. He told you that this child would be a living testimony of God's mercy and many souls would be converted at the telling of their story. He told you that they would prosper in all that they do and that the yoke of poverty on your family would be broken with the anointing that would rest in them. With that it seems that the more you hear these words about your baby, the worse he gets. He's running with gangs or selling drugs, promiscuity has a stronghold on his life and it does not look good for him at all.

Through all of this, belief and expectancy in you is increasing, which by definition can be faith OR fear.

SCENARIO ONE

You have faith and believe that your God cannot fail and that the words He spoke over the life of your seed cannot and will not return void. You see your child running to the altar and giving his life to Christ. You see God using the boldness and aggressiveness that the devil has had a field day with, and using it to snatch souls out of the kingdom of darkness for His glory. For we walk by faith. Not by sight! This is the exercising of your faith. Now faith is the substance of things hoped for, the evidence or the living proof of things not seen. (Hebrews11: 1, with my emphasis) So with your eyes you don't see it, but in your heart you believe and your expectation is of the Lord. Because you know that everything He's ever spoken in times past has come to pass, you need only wait for the physical manifestation and praise God for it until it happens. The more you praise, the better you feel. The better you feel, the easier it is for you to exercise your faith. The more you exercise your faith, the stronger your faith becomes. The stronger your faith becomes the more you praise. The more you praise, the more God is compelled to move into your circumstance and find Himself where you are because the Lord inhabits or takes up residence in your praise. Before you know it, chains are being broken not only in your child's life, but in every area of your own life. Deliverances are coming and manifestation of prophecies are popping up everywhere because where the Spirit of the Lord is - in your praise, which has increased because of your increasing faith - there is liberty (freedom, no bondage)! Life changing things happen because of properly placed expectation. This is your FAITH IN ACTION!

SCENARIO TWO

You are afraid. You know what God said but this child is getting worse and worse. You believe that because of all of the things your child is doing that death and destruction is their certain end. "Maybe the preacher didn't hear God clearly when he prophesied to me." You cannot sleep at night because you live in fear waiting for that midnight call telling you to come to the hospital. You worry that the knock at the door from the police is inevitable. You are afraid that the aggressiveness and boldness in your child is going to walk him into a situation that he will not be able to fight his way out of and land him in an early grave. *Fear took hold upon them there, and pain, as of a woman in travail* (Psalm 48:6). This is the exercising of your fear. So although none of these things have happened, you convince yourself and your expectation is in the worst possible outcome. Because the child's father was that way or you live in a terrible neighborhood and statistics say that it is more likely that your baby will go to jail than go to college and everyone that your child has been running with has either been killed, nearly killed or gone to jail and they still haven't changed. So you prepare your mind to be strong and brace yourself for the worst so when it does hit you won't break. You praise Satan for his works by complaining and speaking the negativity of your situation. The more you complain the worse you feel. The worse you feel the easier it gets for you to expect or believe bad things are destined to happen. The more you expect bad things to happen the stronger your fears become. The stronger your fear becomes the more you complain and speak out of fear. The more you speak out of that fear the more authority you give to the enemy to usher himself into your situation and stay there because Satan receives his authority when you praise his works by speaking negative words into your life and your atmosphere. Before you know it, terrible things begin to happen, not only in the life of your child but now even in your own life. Destruction is all around and the words that you spoke out of your own mouth are beginning to manifest right before your eyes. Because where the spirit of fear is - which is not just in your heart and mind but has now overtaken your life and been spoken out of your mouth in the form of murmuring and complaining or satanic praise, which has increased because of your increasing fear - there is bondage (no deliverance, no happy ending)! Life changing things happen because of improperly placed expectation. This is your FEAR IN ACTION!

For those of you who require dissection with the tool of a certified expert let's look a little closer.

Faith as defined in Webster's New World Dictionary and Thesaurus is *unquestioning belief or EXPECTATION specifically in God or a religion, complete trust or confidence, loyalty.*

The thesaurus breaks it down further as *assurance, credence, acceptance, truth, sureness certainty, reliance and conviction.* It then offers these words as antonyms or opposite meanings of *faith*: *doubt, suspicion, distrust.*

Fear as defined in Webster's New World Dictionary and Thesaurus is *to be afraid; to EXPECT with misgiving (doubt).*

The thesaurus further defines fear as *suspicion, doubt, mortal terror, panic, misgiving, phobia, timidity.* The opposite meaning of fear is *courage* when used as a noun. As a verb (or action) fear is *to avoid, lose courage or live in terror* with the antonym, or opposite meaning, being *to dare, outface or withstand.*

All of the words in these definitions are connected or related in some way. By definition alone, you can see that whether you walk in faith or walk in fear, you are walking in EXPECTATION. All that means is that the same thing you need to do to have faith in God and in His word and His promises, is the same thing you need to do to believe that bad things will happen, which seems to be very easy for most people. Without even trying, most people will believe it when they hear something negative and often times will believe it without proof that it exists or is true. Hmm ... believing something without proof of its existence sounds like faith to me. It just seems as though most of us have been pointing our faith in the wrong direction.

You can have faith in God! Unmovable, unshakable, mountain-moving, life-changing faith! One of the biggest tricks that the enemy has been able to play on the minds of the saints is making them believe that their faith cannot be strong enough for the big things or the hard things. Because we won't even attempt to believe for certain things, there are some areas of our lives in which the enemy is already triumphing. The good news for you is that it does not have to stay this way. I believe I have shown you today that you already posses the ingredients to have fearless faith. All you need to do is change the direction of your expectation, move from the negative to the positive and begin building your faith. The more faith you have, the less fear you have.

Visualize it as a number line like the ones we used to get in math class.

EXPECTATION GRAPH

FEAR   FAITH

-9 -8 -7 -6 -5 -4 -3 -2 -1 0 1 2 3 4 5 6 7 8 9 10 11

0

Bad diagnosis is issued from the doctor, prognosis is bleak, word of prophecy comes forth proclaiming healing

-1 I know God can heal but I saw the x-ray.

+1 This is hard but if healing is possible, it's only possible with God, so I trust Him.

-2 I'll start treatment. Doctor says this may help. I don't want to die.

+2 I'll start treatment and believe God to do what He said. I shall live and not die and declare the works of the Lord!

Joined patient support group. Met a lady who told me how she's planning her funeral and getting her affairs in order just in case. She offers to help me get connected to the patient services people who will help me do the same with my own affairs at little or no cost to me.

-6 I listen and let her walk me through the process. You never know what could happen and there's nothing wrong with being prepared, "just in case". This is depressing me.

+6 We talk and I begin to tell her about the special prayer at my church for healing. I invite her to come and she does. She accepts Christ as her savior and I have a new friend. This is exciting me!

EXPECTATION GRAPH

FEAR   **FAITH**

-9   -8   -7   -6   -5   -4   -3   -2   -1   0   1   2   3   4   5   6   7   8   9   10   11

0

I found out recently that there is a history of this disease in my family. Most of the older people in my family died from this same disease. The doctor explained to me that it is generational and in my family we have a greater chance of becoming afflicted with this sickness. There are some preventative measures to lessen the chances, but this is something that will affect not only me but will most likely affect my children and their children and on and on.

-7 This was going to happen no matter what. Maybe it came a little earlier with me than it did with grandma but nothing was going to stop it from coming anyway. The family needs to know this so they can watch for signs in themselves. They may have a better chance if they catch it early. Church services are becoming too tiring to sit through. I don't need to be there that much now. I've put my time in. Besides, I'm tired and they know I'm sick.

+ 7 The devil is a liar! This is war. So now you want to try and tell me that my kids and theirs will have to endure this nonsense? I think not! Not only am I coming forth completely healed, but the cycle stops with me and goes no further. I need to alert the intercessors at church and let them know that I need the warriors with me on this one! I press to attend service and when I'm there, God does something for me every time. I leave rejuvenated. Doctor says he's never seen anything like it.

EXPECTATION GRAPH

FEAR   FAITH

-9 -8 -7 -6 -5 -4 -3 -2 -1 0 1 2 3 4 5 6 7 8 9 10 11

0

-8 Treatments are taking their toll and I'm getting weaker. There are no real signs of improvement. I'm spending a lot of time at home and don't make too many services. I'm afraid. I am grateful I met a friend and I can talk to her because she understands what I'm going through. But she's not doing too well either.

Lord, I don't understand? Why me?

-9 I look terrible. I feel worse, I'm barely mobile and I have accepted that this is the way my life will end. I am in pain and I just want it to go away. My family is suffering. My new friend died and I have just left her funeral. I watched her suffer. I'm suffering and I have seen what lies ahead for me. Lord I'm tired.

+8 Treatments are going well. Some days I feel better than others, but I know it's already done. Doctor says he looks forward to my visits. I bring sunshine to the office. He says I have all his patients talking about healing. My new friend is seeing marked improvement in her case. Her whole family has started coming to church with her. She's looking for places to go on vacation as soon as she can begin traveling again.

-9 Treatments are done. I look healthy. I'm feeling better. The x-rays came back clean. My friend is healed and will be leaving for Hawaii soon. She's always wanted to go there. Her family joined the church. We're all rejoicing. Her family is rejoicing. My family is rejoicing and everyone is planning for the next phase of life.

EXPECTATION GRAPH

FEAR   FAITH

-9 -8 -7 -6 -5 -4 -3 -2 -1 0 1 2 3 4 5 6 7 8 9 10 11

0

-10 Death comes and a family is left devastated. The opportunity to save not only lives but souls was missed. Two families lost dear ones because fear caused words and actions that empowered it not only to steal their lives, but also to continue to invade the family. A seed of fear has been planted in the lives of the children and spreads among the family members of this ugly disease. The cycle moves now to the next generation to be broken.

-10 Life has been restored and souls have been won! Generational curses have been broken. Instead of eulogies being read, testimonies are being given and the faith in this one person sparks an outbreak of faith that sweeps through the family and the church!

When your expectation is of the worst there is no disappointment in your outcome because what you believe you receive, you shall have!

When your expectation is of the Lord there is no disappointment in your outcome because we know that all things work together for good to them that love the Lord and are called according to His purpose. (SEE ROMANS 8:28)

Remember whether it's negatively established (FEAR) or positively established (FAITH), you will get exactly what you expected to receive!

Chapter Ten
THE TRUTH ABOUT FAITH

The same faith that can heal a headache heals cancer.

The same faith you need to get $20, you need to get $20 million. To God it's just a number. If you don't have $20 for bus fare to get to and from work until payday, you'll find a way to get it. You may even mumble a prayer and say, "Lord, where will I get bus fare this week?" You may call and borrow it or remember that someone owes it to you. The point is, you devise a plan, move on it and have faith that you are going to get that $20. You have to get it because you have to go to work! Even if you get it piece by piece, just enough to go back and forth every day, you make it. If you wanted $20 million, the process is the same. You need to consult God first and then devise a good plan. In fact when you speak to God about it He will show you how to do it. Then you need to get to work on it. It may all come at one time or in increments, but it will come when your faith is put into action. The problem is that many of you would never even think to go to God, put your faith to work and say, "Lord, I need You to give me a God idea or a witty invention that will change my life and pour wealth into me forever." Could you believe that? Or is it easier for you to believe that you could sooner lose your job, go broke, have to file for bankruptcy and start life all over again, not at the bottom of the barrel but underneath it?

What would happen if for every time you set your mind to believe something negative you repositioned your thoughts and started faith talking the very opposite of what is in front of you? There is a song that I used to sing as a young girl growing up in church. The words to the song said *I'm looking for a miracle, I expect the impossible, I feel the intangible, I've seen the invisible* and it continues to say, *the sky is the limit to what I can have, I expect a miracle everyday!* It was one of the most popular gospel songs of that time and everywhere you went, people were singing it. It was so popular that people who didn't go to church would sing this song! I think about it now and I ask myself, "Do we as Christians even listen to the things we sing about? Do we really pay attention to the things that speak out of our mouths? Good or bad?" The answer, sadly, is NO! Most of us really don't expect a miracle everyday, although we are entitled to one everyday. That means that a whole lot of us who consider ourselves deep in the spirit really don't have a walk of faith like we say we do. If we did, our lives would reflect more victory than they do presently.

FAITH CHECK. Do you expect to go to work today and have that supervisor or co-worker get on you nerves like they always do, or do you expect that the Lord is going to work a miracle on your behalf and change the atmosphere on your job so you can have peace throughout the day? Do you prepare to have to go home everyday and fuss with your unruly child about the sneaky things they are doing, or are you expecting that in the next service the spirit of conviction and repentance will over-take them and they will run to the altar? Are you expecting total healing for your body or have you conditioned yourself to just live with the inconvenience of your condition? Do you really believe that you can be made whole emotionally and live to see true forgiveness and reconciliation in your family, or have you set your mind to believe that you don't need anybody but yourself? Just what do you expect? Because it is the very thing you are expecting that determines what you will have. It is the thing that you are expecting which determines and defines whether you have fearless faith or faithless fear. I submit to you that whatever it is you choose to live by, it is all faith. It is faith in your God, which is true faith or it is fear of the negative, which is what I call satanic, or dark, faith.

Do you believe what the Word of God says? Do you believe in the promises of Jesus, or do you believe that nothing good can ever happen for you and that your life was meant to fail? Do you believe that you are destined to repeat the mistakes of your parents, your grandparents and even your own past, or do you believe that you can do all things through Christ who strengthens you? Even overcome the repetition of failure, poverty and depression that has run through generations in your family? I need for you to understand that whatever it is you believe about you is exactly what will be.

There are promises guaranteed to each of you in your life. You have the promises that are guaranteed to come with the road that you would travel in your faith walk - righteousness, peace, joy, prosperity and wholeness in your mind, body and spirit. All of these wonderful attributes belong to you! Then there are the promises that you are guaranteed to receive as a result of walking in fear, unfaith or dark faith - anger, frustration, depression, poverty and sickness of the mind, body and spirit. Even to those who do not walk in Godly faith but may have wealth, will tell you on an honest day that they lack in many or all of these other areas. But why not have it all if you can? As a born-again believer, it is your right to have it all.

When you walk in fear - which is Satan's desire for all of us - there may be remnants or glimpses of the faith walk that he will flash at you or even let you taste but never all of it, because he can't. His job is to convince you that you can live your life any way you want to with no accountability or consideration of others and still have whatever you want. This is so far from the truth. I have said before that for every truth God speaks, the devil speaks a lie. For every real blessing the Lord sends, Satan sends a counterfeit blessing. You can spend counterfeit cash if you want, but remember that even the best looking counterfeit bill gets caught and taken out of circulation eventually.

My point is that the devil may be able to do things like offer you money, but because total wealth isn't within his power, you will lack in other areas. Maybe your health will be poor or your personal relationships with family members will be lacking. Money spends out but wealth is ongoing, so when you think about it - which would you rather have? With Christ you can have it all - love, joy, peace and wealth in your mind, body, spirit and bank account!

If we go back to the contestants on the television show and look for the common characteristic in every winner, it wouldn't be that they were totally fearless. The common characteristic would be that each one set their face toward the prize and decided within themselves that "though fear would present itself to me, I have already conditioned my mind that I have come too far to turn around. I left my family, flew all the way here and called everyone I know and told them to watch the show. I'm on television, there is this prize at the end and it belongs to me if I can just make it through. I'm not the fastest, I'm not the strongest, but I am determined, my mind is conditioned and I refuse to let fear make me turn around." This is the attitude that you must have about everything in your life.

What is it that you have given up on?

Maybe it's going back to school and you think you're too old or you won't be able to keep up or you can't afford it. Maybe it's getting out of that rental space and owning your own home or office building or maybe it's finally going out on a limb, quitting that job and starting your own business, but fear is holding you hostage. Maybe you have decided that you have been hurt too many times and you refuse to give love a chance to come to you again. Don't allow fear or dark faith to keep you from living life whole and having everything that belongs to you.

Fear is crippling. Faith is strengthening. Fear keeps you in the dark. Faith leads you to the light. Fear breaks you. Faith makes you whole.

SURROUND YOURSELF WITH FAITH
Don't fool yourself and think that it requires a lot of faith. God knows that we are human and He knows how easy it is to get swayed by things that are

thrown right before our faces. He doesn't expect you to start off with faith the size of a mountain. Instead, He has created a miracle in itself – He has made the provision that if your faith can only be as big as a mustard seed (the smallest seed of all seeds), you can move mountains (mountain-sized issues or problems) with it.

Take your mustard seed faith and give it to God. Your little becomes much when you place it in God's hands. Not just the tangible things in your life but the intangibles as well - like your faith.

Lastly, when you find yourself growing weary and losing faith, get with someone who can encourage you to keep holding on. Latch on to someone who is going to help keep your faith built up with his or her own until you are strong enough to stand on yours again.

If you go back to the diagram, on the FEAR side you will see that a big part of the problem with the two patients was they reinforced each other's doubts and fears and as a result they helped each other along, right to the grave! They had each other for support but they spoke words of negativity. They shared their expectations of the bad with one another and it latched on and helped expedite death in their lives. Souls missed Heaven and the generational curse lived on to continue to torture the family.

However, when you look on the FAITH side of the diagram, you see where words of encouragement came into play. They attended church services together and the faith that started in one individual latched on to the other individual and swept through both families. Souls were added to the kingdom of Heaven, healing came and a curse of sickness that was meant to wipe out a lineage was stopped in its tracks!

You must learn to surround yourself with the right people. I had a very close friend some years ago and we did everything together. We talked about everything good and bad. I began going to intercessory prayer at my church, seeking God for ways to bring change in my life. God revealed to me that I needed to stop talking so much about the negative things in my life because I was giving them life and empowering them with my words. He showed me that the same mouth I used to rehash the devil's mess should be used to bring forth the blessings of God in my life. He also let me know that although He'd blessed me with a friend that was truly my friend, He was not pleased with the conversations we shared. Rather than complaining to each other, we needed to pray together and keep each other lifted. The Lord showed me where we were becoming detriments to each other in our faith walk. He wanted to do something miraculous for us both, but it would require a change in our expectation. This would require a change in our conversation. I shared this with my friend and invited her to begin coming with me to intercessory prayer. She came once, but found reasons every week after that not to come again. As I was going, God began to change my view of some things and even began to change the way I talked about things that were going on in my life. Because my dear friend was not involving herself in prayer with me, I could feel us growing apart. We didn't speak the same language and our conversation was no longer complimentary to each other. Our relationship is not what it was and, although I know we still love each other dearly, there will come a time when the Lord will speak and when He does, you must obey. Anything and anyone that is not moving in the direction that the Lord tells you to move in must be left behind. Your life may depend on it.

Speak it out of your mouth and watch it come to pass. This is the expectation of those who believe and those who do not believe. Faith for all that is good and of God. Fear for all that is negative and of the enemy.

Chapter Eleven
YOU'RE PREGNANT WITH A PROMISE

I'd like to give you another example of how to work your faith and how your faith, in turn, will work for you. I'm driving this point so hard because the truth is, you already posses the strength, agility and portion of confidence that it takes to receive a hard thing or a miracle using your inner expectation mechanism. I have already shown you that it is faith - just faith pointed in the wrong direction. God has made you many promises. He wants to bring every one of them to pass. Satan does not have the authority to stop the promise of God in your life. He does however, have a very slick and cunning way of making you talk yourself out of your blessing. He is the ultimate mind-gamer! Don't listen to him! Don't believe what he says to you. Your promises are the same. God has not changed His mind about you. You must rehearse the promises of God for your life over and over again so it will connect with your spirit. You must then begin to act like someone who is expecting for the promise to take place. Get ready for it. Make the necessary preparations. Would you hand someone $10 million who doesn't have a bank account to put it in? Or worse, would you give that kind of money to someone who doesn't see the need to have a bank account? I have said it before - faith is action. Your level of faith is openly seen and known according to what it is you begin to do after receiving a word of promise from God. Your expectation must be in the right direction and with that comes preparation - taking actions that say, "I am ready to receive what God promised me." If the devil can keep you looking and aiming your faith in the wrong direction, you will never live the life of abundance that God has planned and promised for you to live.

Take the woman who is pregnant. She's received this wonderful news from her doctor and now she's given instructions on how to take care of her body while she is *expecting* or *waiting in faith* for the arrival of her baby. Waiting in faith for the baby means eating the right foods, taking her prenatal vitamins and iron, making all of her doctor's appointments, avoiding stress, staying away from people who are sick, picking a name for the baby, buying baby furniture and clothes, maybe even enrolling in Lamaze classes. She's happy and in celebration mode. Friends and family believe and expect and are celebrating her promise as well by giving her a baby shower. Throughout the expectation period there are good days and not-so-good days because sometimes there is morning sickness or backaches, maybe even a little cramping. There may even be more serious times during the course of the pregnancy where there is spotting or the threat of miscarrying. It is during these times that the expectant mother keeps in touch with the doctor daily - sometimes several times a day - and does everything he tells her to do. She continues to keep a good spirit and believe that this baby is going to be alright. She talks to her belly and calls the baby by its name and tells the baby that you are going to come at the appointed time. Not prematurely and not late.

NOTE* *It is dangerous for a baby to come too early and it is a danger for a baby to be held in the womb too long after its full term has been reached. Either situation can mean severe handicap, retardation or even death to the baby.****

She lets nothing, not even the threat of a miscarriage; turn her faith in the other direction. She lets nothing take away the expectation of her promise. Circumstances may look grim but she believes what the doctor told her the result of this pregnancy would be, so she keeps doing all of the necessary things to prepare for the promise. She doesn't have long now and she knows if she can just hold on, she's going to birth the promise. Now the time has come. The baby is fully developed and must be brought forth.

She's knows she's done all of the right things and taken good care of herself. Now labor begins. Labor is grueling but the pain is her only indication that her body is ready to expel the baby and push it out into the world. The labor is sometimes long and intense but there's no turning back at this point. This is the final stage of the expectation period before this baby comes into the world. Ironically this is also the most painful time of the entire pregnancy, but the mother knows she must endure the pain to bring the baby into the world.

NOTE *Every birthing process is a near death experience. There is a literal tearing of the insides of her body in order to give birth so it is the closest that a woman will come to death during her life. However this tearing and extreme pain is necessary to bring forth life****

The pain is great and the mother wants to push, but instead she focuses and listens for the voice of her doctor to give instructions. Although there may be others in the delivery room, she will hear no other voice but the voice of her doctor because she knows he's the only one that can help her get through the delivery safely with a healthy baby. Finally, the doctor tells her to push. She grits her teeth, bears down and pushes. The head crowns. She hears the doctor again and she pushes. Now the neck and shoulders are out. She's excited and impatient all at the same time and she goes to push and the doctor says NO! Wait, don't push! This is uncomfortable. There may be a series of stop and go with the pushing but the mother follows every instruction to the letter because she trusts her doctor and she knows if she doesn't deviate from his plan, it is guaranteed that neither she nor the baby is harmed during the delivery. But after much patience and suffering through the pain, there is a release and the mother is told to give one more push. She gives birth to a healthy baby. The result of her expectation has come forth, the promise has been kept and joy has been brought into her life. WHAT A WONDERFUL OUTCOME!

This is not always the case. Sometimes the baby remains in the womb past its term and labor has to be induced by the doctor to bring the baby out.

There are times when the end result of a pregnancy is not the birth of a healthy baby. Sometimes the baby is premature because the condition of the womb is turbulent and not conducive to the development of a healthy baby. Or the instructions that were given to the mother during her pregnancy were not followed. This results in the baby having to be incubated and cared for by the doctor and his staff so it can be nursed until it is healthy enough to be given to the mother to care for. Sometimes the premature baby will catch up with other full term babies and be healthy with no lasting effects of the near-fatal delivery. Then there are the times that the baby survives, but is never as healthy or fully-developed as other children the same age. Then there are the most tragic instances of all - abortion, miscarriage and stillbirth. Abortion is the decision to destroy any possibility of the birth of the baby. This happens usually in instances when the expectant mother is unhappy, unwilling or feels incapable of caring for the baby so she chooses not to have it.

Miscarriage is another result of a baby trying to grow in an environment that is nonconductive to its healthy development. Miscarriages are extremely painful. They are more painful than the actual birthing process because the pregnant body was intended to go through the process and bring forth life. When it is interrupted in the midst of the process this unintended and unnatural happening causes intense physical pain and then extreme mental distress because the woman is forced to deal with the fact that her expectancy has been terminated and has brought forth sorrow and no baby.

Stillbirths are the final, and in my opinion, the most tragic of all of the outcomes of an unsuccessful pregnancy. A pregnancy that results in a baby being stillborn is only after the mother has carried the baby many times to full term. She walks around every day with this child in her. She has told all her family and friends, possibly even picked out names and had a baby shower. She's felt the child move and kick yet in the end she delivers a dead baby (promise). WHAT A TRAGEDY!

What happened? In both instances, the doctor spoke the promise of a baby and there was expectation. Was he wrong? That expectation was either followed with obedience to the instructions of the doctor and a cheery disposition, or disobedience and a negative attitude toward the promise. Depending on what the promise of the baby was surrounded and developed with determined the outcome of the pregnancy.

Do you see yourself here? When God (the doctor) brings you the good news and speaks a promise/blessing (the baby) over your life, you must move in the direction of the promise. Start preparing for the arrival of your blessing. Whatever steps are necessary - take them. Keep a cheery disposition. Don't allow negative things to enter your spirit. Feed yourself with good food (the word of God and songs of praise) so your promise can grow healthy and strong within you. Talk to it. Sing about it. There are times when the enemy may try and make you get discouraged and abort the thing God told you is yours. Fight him! Keep your expectation moving in the right direction. There are times when Satan will literally try to rob you of your promise and force you to miscarry. You don't have to miscarry. Call on the Lord (the doctor), bombard Heaven several times a day and await His instructions. Keep doing what you already know to do, say, "though this threat exists, the Lord says I will deliver and I BELIEVE GOD!" You'll make it past that stage and, before you know it, you will reach term and labor pains will begin. You find yourself experiencing the strongest and most intense trials of your Christian walk. It feels like you are going to die! Don't give up! Listen for the voice of the Lord. It would be no greater pleasure to the devil than to have you get to the point of delivery and have you deliver a dead promise or even kill yourself in the process because you pushed too soon. Remember that in order to bring forth the promise, you must endure the labor. As you listen, you'll hear the prompting of your Father saying, "PUSH! It's not easy, but PUSH! I can see the head crowning, PUSH!" There may even come a time when you have to slow down and stop pushing for the safety of the promise and yourself, but trust in God and remember He is not slack concerning His promises but must bring to pass everything that He speaks out of His mouth concerning you! Eventually you will hear Him tell you to resume pushing all the way through the safe and healthy delivery of the promise He spoke over you.

The expectation mechanism already exists in each and every one of us. You decide how it will be used and for what purpose. When God speaks a word over your life, it is a sure thing - just like when the doctor tells you that you are pregnant, it is a sure thing. The promise and the baby are both already planted and growing. You have to know that it's there so you can take proper care of yourself (the mother, the carrier of the promise) and prepare for the arrival. It's up to you. You can take your human expectation and point it in the wrong direction and allow fear to over take you and bring you a tragic outcome, or you can turn that expectation into Godly faith and start moving in the direction of your promise and receive a bouncing (baby) blessing at the end of your spiritual pregnancy!

I am confident that I have successfully aided in awaking your inner expectation mechanism and you can now turn it and use it as faith. Now I just need you to take the limit off of God and believe that He can do exceedingly and abundantly above anything you could ever even ask or think! Your imagination could never be bigger than the one who gave you the ability to imagine. Your creativity could never out-create the one who gave you the ability to create.

SECTION III
Praise: For Life

Chapter Twelve
ANOINTED TO PRAISE

If I were to take a poll among a number of people with any knowledge of praise and the great leaders of the Bible and any connection between the two and ask the question, "Who was the greatest praiser to ever live?" From preacher to pew warmer, without a doubt they'd all say with certainty that it was David. From Bible scholar to Sunday school student, we all recognize the name David as being synonymous with praise. David was anointed to praise. Through all of David's imperfections, flaws and even his sinful acts, David found that he could always get an audience with God through his praise. He mastered the art of getting God's attention even when he was as wrong as two left shoes. Yes, David was anointed to praise. There has not been such a praiser since that time, but the ability remains for many to rise and to learn the skill and the art of praise. A lot of you will not agree with that because it messes with your theology. In your mind there was one David and there will never be another. I can and do agree that there was one David and will never be another, however, I believe that through our spiritual DNA comes not just the ability but the opportunity to become a praise phenomenon! How? I'm glad you asked!

Chapter Thirteen
PRAISE=ENERGY, ENERGY=PRAISE

Praise is glorified, divinely empowered energy put out from our beings (our mouths and bodies) for the purpose of uplifting the savior. (That is my definition, Webster has his own.) Praise requires movement of some sort, whether it's your mouth or your body combined with energy. A cold-blooded praise is accomplished by completely removing yourself from your circumstance, no matter what it is (but particularly in a time of great trial or tribulation), forgetting the environment, your present surroundings, and the people around you so that you may completely lose yourself in praise. A cold-blooded praise involves moving every part of your body that can be moved, combined with as much energy as you can physically give.

David was anointed in this area of high-energy praise. David was a cold-blooded praiser. He gave God high-energy praise every time he got the chance. Notice, I keep connecting the word *energy* in my definitions and examples of praise. I do this on purpose. Here's why:

> The word *energy* means *the capacity for doing work* (that *is* Miriam Webster's definition).

Please allow me to take you back a few years to Earth Science class for a moment. I remember in high school when we learned about the different kinds of energy (potential, kinetic, thermal, electrical, nuclear, etc.). We learned that although there were many different types of energy, two things remained constant for all forms - 1) it never dies and, 2) all forms of energy are associated with motion. According to the laws of energy, it is neither created nor destroyed. Energy is only transferred. Energy is in the Earth and in the Earth's atmosphere. It has been since creation. God put it here and wrapped it up in the laws of nature and sent it on its assignment and it has been hard at work in the Earth ever since.

Think about it - what is the first thing you do if you walk into a room where someone is depressed, laying in the dark, and you want to lift their spirits? You start turning on lights, moving things around, raising your voice and opening up windows to bring some energy to their atmosphere. Rainy days are draining, and for the most part many people can sleep through a rainy day or be lazy and relaxed and not want to leave the house. But if the sun is out, most people can't sleep, even if they are tired. We have to get busy and get things done. We have to hit the streets! The sun gives energy and makes us want to move and be active.

This same energy present in the Earth's atmosphere is also present in praise (or this divinely empowered energy) and has been imparted and passed down through generations, even though most have not used it. I told you that energy doesn't die; it only transfers from one form to another and one being to another. That means that this energy, this capacity for doing work, this praise - no matter how long it has laid dormant - is here and has the *potential* to be stirred up.

Potential Energy is *energy deriving from position*. I have good news for you, you are already in position because of your status as an heir to the wealth of praise passed down by David. Even if your body is at rest, you are able to tap into this anointing and become what David was because you have potential energy. The goal is to get you to move from potential energy to **kinetic energy**. Any moving body has kinetic energy. Let me remind you that because energy is never destroyed but only transferred, you can move into this anointing a lot easier than you believe. What happens during the transfer of energy? Energy is designated according to its nature. In simplified terms, that means when the energy is transferred from one object or being to the next, the capacity of work that is applied determines how that energy will manifest itself. What has happened with this anointed energy to praise that was passed on by our forefather David, is that because no one believed that they could parallel or exceed David in praise, no one has taken up the praise mantle and it has passed from a state of kinetic energy to a state of rest - or potential energy.

The good news for us is that in spite of it not being used, it was passed down! So even if those who have gone before us didn't know they had it, or didn't accept the inheritance and multiply it, we can do it ourselves here and now. Thank God we have hope!

For those of you who are willing to put in some work, you have the ability to change that *potential energy* into *kinetic energy* and take your rightful place as the descendant of David, as the heir of praise, and with your covenant right, posses your inheritance so that your life may be richer, so that the struggle of life may be eased in some areas and completely erased in others.

Receive your inheritance as the seed of David so that your present can be filled with promise and your future will be filled with the manifestation of those promises. This must be because you will have grown the wealth to leave the inheritance for your natural and spiritual seed.

The songwriter tried to get us to grasp it when he said:

> *Blessed assurance, Jesus is mine. Oh what a foretaste of glory divine!*
> *Heir of salvation purchased by God, born of his spirit, washed in his blood.*
> *This is my story, this is my song. Praising my savior all the day long!*
> *This is my story, this is my song. Praising my savior all the day long!*

Seize this wealth of praise and teach it to the next generation so that you can live your life with the *blessed assurance* that because you have left an inheritance for your children's children, they will want for nothing. This is your assurance and it becomes your insurance because God can deny a praiser nothing!

Why deny what is rightfully yours? It came from your daddy! IT'S IN YOUR DNA!!!

Chapter Fourteen
THE DAVID CONNECTION

IT'S IN YOUR GENES

We as Christians often refer to ourselves as the seed of Abraham. We are a part of his lineage. We have his DNA. Now, especially in this time of awareness, when many of us are realizing for the first time in our much sanctified lives that as the seed of Abraham, God never intended for us to be poor and needy. So we migrate to the teachings that confirm that we are covenant children. We hold fast to the teachings that we are the seed of Abraham and, as such, we have the right to stake our claim to all the wonderful blessings and promises that God made Abraham in Genesis chapter 17.

And when A'bram was ninety years old and nine, the Lord appeared unto A'bram, and said unto him, I am the Almighty God; walk before me, and be thou perfect. And I will make my covenant between me and thee, and will multiply thee exceedingly. And A'bram fell on his face: and God talked with him, saying, as for me, behold, my covenant is with thee, and thou shalt be a father of many nations. Neither shall thy name any more be called A'bram, but thy name shall be Abraham; for a father of many nations I have made thee. And I will make thee exceeding fruitful, and I will make nations of thee, and kings shall come out of thee. And I will establish my covenant between me and thee and thy seed after thee in their generations for an everlasting covenant, to be a God unto the, and to thy seed after thee.
And God said unto Abraham, Thou shalt keep my covenant therefore, thou, and thy seed after thee in their generations.
GENESIS 17:1-7, 9

That was a good word!! A sure word. One that - from the time it was spoken - has been established in the Earth and in the lives of all those who received it and kept covenant accordingly with the Father. This makes perfect sense because we know that there was nothing poor or needy about Abraham. So now that this truth has been established in our minds and has taken root in our hearts and spirits, many of us are in hot pursuit of the prosperity that we are entitled to because of the covenant that God made with Abraham generations ago. But is that all? Does it end there? If we are indeed the heirs to this great and wonderful promise, if we really do possess the DNA of Abraham and he is our father, if you and I truly are the rightful recipients of this rich heritage and legacy, shouldn't this mean that there are other things in the lineage that we have the right to claim ownership to? Things other than prosperity in our finances? Isn't David a part of the lineage of Abraham? Yes he is!

The book of the generation of Jesus Christ, the son of David, the son of A'braham.
MATTHEW 1:1

That would, like Abraham, make David our father, which entitles us to receive the wealth that he left behind. Most of us are extremely small minded and our problem is that when we hear "inheritance," our minds automatically shift to thoughts of "our cut." Our minds go straight to the thought of money and finances. I somewhat understand that, since traditionally when loved-ones die, they leave money or things of value for their family members who survive them. But understand this, they do so with the hope that what they left for their successors or survivors would be taken and used wisely and even multiplied so that the struggle of life is eased or removed. In some cases, the wishes of the deceased are carried out, the wealth is preserved and multiplied and life gets better for the original heir and for generation after generation in the family's lineage. In other cases what has been left gets squandered and used unwisely. It isn't multiplied or preserved for those generations to follow. The tools to maintain and grow wealth are never passed on, and, as a result, after only a minimal period of enjoyment with the inheritance by the original heirs -

all of the wealth is gone and subsequent generations find themselves poor and destitute and usually in a worse state than when they started.

The Bible says in Proverbs that:
A good man leaveth an inheritance for his children's children: and the wealth of the sinner is laid up for the just.
PROVERBS 13:22

David left a wealth of praise in the family lineage for his descendants to grab hold of and multiply it in the Earth so that our struggle in life would be eased and - in some areas - completely removed. Praise has the power to remove struggle! Yet we live with struggle and accept it everyday and tell ourselves that it's just a part of life. There are some things that we must endure for a season and then overcome it for a testimony of deliverance to someone else who will need to hear it. But just to sit down passively and accept that every new height in life that we aim for has to be a struggle? I THINK NOT!

Our father David understood this. Just as our father Abraham understood that his children would never have to live life forsaken or begging bread.

I have been young, and now am old; yet have I not seen the righteous forsaken, nor his seed begging bread.
PSALM 37:25

Abraham could die in peace because he knew that God had promised him that his seed would be exceedingly fruitful forevermore. Many of us today don't have that peace of mind. And although we aren't afraid for what will happen to our souls when we die, we do worry about what will become of our children or our spouses and loved ones when we die. Why? Because we have no assurances of their well-being if we are not here to take care of them. Some Pastors are afraid for their ministries and churches because they have no assurances of what will happen after they are gone. That's no way to live. Wouldn't it be worth it for you to know that you had the ability to get some assurances concerning your life and then pass that on to your natural and spiritual seed? Just as we have the covenant right to claim the blessings of our father Abraham for our lives, we not only have the covenant right but the responsibility to claim the inheritance of praise left to us by our father David. It's in our DNA! If we could open our minds and receive this revelation and let it take root in our spirits, we would keep demons running from us. The powerful praise that David carried in the deepest parts of his spirit did not die when he died. There are undeveloped Davids all over the world, and because we refuse to believe that anyone could ever become as great a praiser as David, we won't even reach for it.

Again I'm going to mess with some of your theology with this one. Not only can you be as great a praiser as David, but you have the ability and the potential to be a greater praiser than David ever was!

JOHN 5:19-20
(19) Then answered Jesus and said unto them Verily, verily I say unto you, the son can do nothing of himself but what he seeth the father do: for what things soever he doeth these also doeth the son likewise (20) for the father loveth the son and showeth him all things that himself doeth and he will show him greater works that ye may marvel.

JOHN 14:12
Verily, verily I say unto you, He that believeth on me, the works that I do shall he do also; AND GREATER WORKS THAN THESE SHALL HE DO because I go to my father.

Simply put, the great works of our fathers were examples for us to learn and then do, and not only to do, but do even better than our fathers.

Even Jesus said that we would do greater works than He did while He was here on Earth. The only qualification needed, according to this scripture reference, is to believe in Him. He had to leave and go back to His father but the work needed to continue and grow. We know the great miracles and works He performed during His short lifetime, so how much more can we do in ours? The same principal applies with praise, as shown to us by David. So if David our father gave us an example of what real praise that touches the very heart of God is, and went down in history as the greatest praiser to ever live, then there is a vacant position waiting to be filled by a descendant of his. His work must also continue and grow.

Will it be you?

This principal is not just for things of a spiritual nature but can and should also be applied to matters of everyday life.

Chapter Fifteen
THERE IS FREEDOM IN YOUR PRAISE

Let everything that hath breath praise the Lord, praise ye the Lord.
PSALM 150:6

THERE IS FREEDOM IN YOUR PRAISE!

God loves to receive praise from His people. The angels sit at the throne of God and worship Him without ceasing, but there is something extra special to God when we, His creation, offer up the sacrifice of praise. Why? Because unlike the angels, we have a free will. The angels sit at the throne and worship because that is what they were created for, they cannot divert from it, they have no choice. But we, God's prize creation and the apple of His eye, were given the wonderful gift of free will. We have the ability and the freedom to say at anytime, "I will praise God now, I will glorify my savior, I will honor Him for his goodness, I will bless Him for his kindness, I will offer up thanksgiving, Hallelujah to my savior!" Yet most of us spend more time giving excuses. "I'm tired," "I don't feel well" or even worse "I don't feel like it." Too often what happens is we allow our feelings or the mood of the moment to get in the way and we don't praise God like we should, not realizing that by holding back our praise we are holding up our breakthrough.

The Bible tells us that God inhabits, or lives in, the praises of His people. The Bible also tells us that where the Spirit of the Lord is, there is liberty. So when you open your mouth and give God an unselfish, uninhibited, unbridled, all the way live praise, He steps down from His throne, comes to where you are and literally pulls up a LazyBoy and reclines in the midst of your praise. That's right, it sounds comical but when you go all out for God in your praise, He says, "this is where I want to be. I'm gonna chill out here with my child for a while since she's gone out of her way to make such comfortable accommodations for me." And guess what? If He's chillin' in your midst He brought liberty and freedom with Him because, again, where the spirit of the Lord is … THERE IS LIBERTY! You can praise your way into freedom! You have the power to usher breakthrough in to your own life. Praise God and chains will begin to fall off.

THE P&S EFFECT

Undoubtedly, there are times in life when this kind of praise seems nearly impossible. The dark times, the midnights of our lives, make this type of praise seem impossible, however, it is at this time when God wants to show Himself mighty in your situation. How do we move God to this point? First we must adopt the "I-have-nothing-to-lose-if-it's-with-my-last-breath-because-He's-worthy-and-if-He-never-does-another-thing-for-me-He's-already-done-more-than-enough-so-I-wont-stop-'til-I-give-Him-some-praise" attitude. Or the abbreviated name that I simply call *the P&S Effect*.

What is the P&S Effect? To fully explain it, I'd have to take you back to the familiar passage in your Bible in the book of Acts (Acts 16:22-36) where we see Paul and Silas on the field teaching, preaching, running revivals, etc. People were being healed, delivered and set free because of the ministry of these obedient servants of God and yet, for their deeds, rather than compensation, accolades or thank-yous, they were set up and reported to the local authorities as lawbreakers. They had their clothes stripped from them by the judges and, in front of a massive crowd, were beat relentlessly while naked, thrown in jail, sent to the inner prison (maximum security) and then locked in the stockades.

So here you have these men of God. All they tried to do was help somebody and they find themselves wrongly accused, naked, bleeding, hurting, hungry, posture bent, hands and feet locked in stocks and shackled, can't get loose and it's the middle of the night. Sounds like you, huh? Enter the P&S Effect:

And at midnight Paul and Silas prayed
And sang praises unto God: and the prisoners heard them.
And suddenly there was a great earthquake,
So that the foundations of the prison were shaken:
And immediately all the doors were opened, and everyone's bands were loosed.
(ACTS 16:25, 26)

Paul and Silas, in the midst of a hurting situation, are physically bound and held captive by their oppressor. It gets to be around midnight and Pastor Paul and Chief Adjutant Silas take inventory of their situation and they began feeling like having a little praise and worship. They took notice that although their hands and feet were bound, their vocal chords were free. They said, "we can't go anywhere" but they decided, "since we're here and they won't let us out we may as well do what we do, right here where we are!" Paul and Silas decided, "let's have a praise party!" They began to cry loud and lift up their voices like trumpets in Zion. They praised God so hard while they were locked in jail that the shackles and chains on their hands and feet fell from them. The stockade that held their hands, feet and head in a crouched-down, head-hung-over, back-bent-out-of-shape position, unlocked itself, opened up and freed them. This praise was so intense that the very foundations of the place of their imprisonment was shaken and the doors of their jail cell, the doors that they could not get to and open for themselves, responded to the sound of their praise and opened up for them. But this was just the beginning of the P & S Effect. Paul and Silas' praise was so powerful that the shackles and stocks of every other prisoner in the inner prison fell from them. The gates of the jail cell of every other prisoner under the sound of their voices unlocked and came open. The atmosphere in that prison changed and the jailer who was sleeping woke up and when he realized what was going on, became afraid,

drew his sword, turned it on himself, about to commit suicide. At that moment, Paul got a word from the Lord for his oppressor and cried out in the darkness and told the jailer, "don't harm yourself, I'm here (we're all here)" and the jailer brought a light into that dark jail cell where Paul and Silas were and with fear and trembling asked them, "what must I do to be saved?" Well you know what happened then. IT WAS ON! Paul ministered the Word of the Lord to his jailer and converted him! After his jailer helped him to clean up all the dirt and blood and sweat from his beatings, Paul baptized him. After which he was invited to the jailer's house for a banquet prepared in his honor. All this and then all the charges were dropped and he was sent away in peace.
THAT'S THE P&S EFFECT!

Can you see your situation yet? Is this you? Are you always trying to help someone and never receive thanks or accolades but rather accusation or misunderstanding of your motives? Do you find yourself imprisoned by character assassinations, other people's opinion of you and lies? Are you shackled in a spiritual stockade and your back is bent over? Is your head hung down? Are you hurting? Is it midnight in your life?

I decree, by the Word of the Lord, that if you - in your depressed, oppressed, rejected, midnight or hurting state - will adopt the attitude of Paul and Silas and tell yourself that in the midst of your trial, "if I can clap my hands or even if I can't clap my hands, if I can stomp my feet or if I can't stomp my feet, if I can wave my hands or if I can't wave my hands and show praise." Whether or not You can do these things if you tell God, "I've got a song just for you and if I can't do anything else Lord, I still have my voice and even if I sound like a frog with laryngitis it's me and You and my song of praise." If you tell yourself, "I'm gonna sing and it doesn't matter who hears me. I'm gonna praise until there's a shift in my atmosphere. I'm going to magnify you Lord, until I shake the foundation of what has me imprisoned. I'm gonna Shabach until my shackles come loose. I'm gonna make noise until others who are bound around me get freed. I will holler until the doors that I've been unable to open for myself come open for me." If you promise the Lord that you will keep yourself open to hear Him so that when the time comes you will be in position to hear a word from Him, even for your enemy, you will be able to deliver a life-saving Rhema word with the compassion of your savior Jesus Christ. If you declare, "I'm gonna praise you, Jesus, until even my enemies and my oppressors acknowledge that You are Lord and You are God and that they need You." Then finally tell Him, "Lord I'm gonna praise You as I help usher my enemies into righteousness and then we will all PRAISE TOGETHER as they help me clean up my wounds (the wounds they have inflicted on me) and the mess (the mess they have caused to rest on me and around me) all before they sit me down to partake in a feast that they have prepared for me to enjoy as I listen to them take back their false accusations and lies and then bless me and tell me to go in Peace!"

Now that's powerful! Its amazing what the Lord can show you through divine revelation of a passage of scripture you've been reading your whole life. Hear what He says. This is the word of the Lord for your situation. If you adopt this attitude, not only will you experience the P & S Effect, but you will infect others around you and start a movement in your home, your communities, your schools, churches and help set this world on fire with praise!

This is not something that is decided based on how many people are going to do it with you. This is, like salvation, an individual decision. The Bible tells us to work out our own soul salvation with fear and trembling. The principle of the P&S Effect is the same. If you, who reads these words, makes up in your mind today that you will adopt the mindset to achieve the P&S Effect, it will make a change in your immediate surroundings and it will catch on like fire!

Paul and Silas didn't have group participation from the other prisoners in the jail when they broke into devotional service at midnight after being battered and abused all day. In fact, I'm sure many of the other prisoners were tired and agitated that they would be so insensitive as to keep everyone else awake after their long day of torture. Yet they made the decision to step out on a limb in the midst of their circumstances. It was a decision made by the two of them that "since this is where I must be, then this is where I must praise!"

The praises of Paul and Silas to their God were so thick that their entire atmosphere became subject to the liberty that was ushered into that place when the Spirit of the Lord showed up and took a seat in the midst of their praise.

You really need to go to the text in your Bible and dissect the Word to understand what was going on so you can get this revelation for yourself. While you are yet in your prison - whatever that may be - and your jailer is sleeping because he's so confident that you are locked up and can't get free, you need to break into a crazy continual praise that will change your atmosphere and free you and all those around you. Then watch your praise open up doors for you that you couldn't get open before. Even before you step out of your prison, you are free because your shackles are off and now you can deliver someone else and walk them out of prison with you.

It's a simple formula. A crazy continual praise will achieve the P & S Effect.

The Bible tells us to offer the sacrifice of praise to God continually, that is the fruit of our lips giving thanks to His name.

What does this mean? This means that not only should you praise hard, but you should praise often — even continually. Praise until your atmosphere changes like Paul and Silas did. Praise until you feel chains breaking from your arms and feet. Praise until the shackles break off of those who are around you. Praise until you feel the shift in your spirit and are empowered. There is power in your praise! Like Paul and Silas in that jail cell you hold the key not only to your own breakthrough, your own deliverance and your own freedom, but you have the power through praise to free those around you as well. This means your disobedient child's strong will must respond to the changes that will take place in your atmosphere when you praise, your money and missing finances must obey and start making its way back home when you praise. Sickness must back up and give room for healing when you praise, brokenness must give way to emotional healing and wholeness when you praise! There is power in your praise! There is liberty in your praise!

Chapter Sixteen
A COLD BLOODED PRAISE

I have talked about the angels who sit at the throne and worship and why it is so special to God to have your praise come to Him and invite Him to where you are. I understand that when you are going through difficult times and facing major challenges in life that it is not easy to put your feelings aside and say, "I'm gonna push past what I feel right now and give God everything I have in praise." But the very fact that your circumstances say that you should be weary and crying and seeking comfort from someone, but you find yourself in praise instead, will move God to do a quick work on your behalf.

Easy? No. Doable? Yes!

Even while facing some of the toughest times in your life, it is imperative that you praise your way through your circumstance. When we go through we have a tendency to question God. We cry out and ask Him, "Lord where are You? Don't hide Your face from me; I need you now more than ever." He's there and waiting to deliver You, but He's also waiting on your praise. I would say to you that God is not looking for you to praise Him *even* when you are going through, but rather *especially* when you are going through. My former Pastor, Bishop Bobby Henderson, has a saying that I love. He tells us at our church that we must, in times of adversity, learn to praise God in cold blood! PRAISE GOD IN COLD BLOOD? That means, "I must develop the mindset of a killer." What could I possibly mean by that?

A cold blooded murderer will gun a person down in broad daylight and not care who sees or knows. A cold blooded killer actually wants someone to see him commit this murder to send a message out that he is not to be messed with. The word will go out even to those who are not around that he is ruthless, compassionless, doesn't care and if you mess with him he'll kill you in cold blood. This is the way we ought to be with our praise. We must graduate to a level of praise that will become so notorious and infamous among our enemies and nay-sayers that people will watch and wonder, "How can he praise God like that? Didn't he just lose his home? Aren't her children strung out? Isn't her marriage breaking up? Didn't they just fire him? "

Your praise ought to be so cold blooded that the Word ought to travel out in the spirit to the very enemy of your soul that if he messes with you, that you will praise God in cold blood, killing the assignment he has placed over your life. The devil himself and all his imps would know that there is a cold blooded praiser on the loose. A cold blooded praiser - one that will praise God in front of anyone at anytime, anywhere, no matter what's going on. Sick in the body - you'll praise, family acting crazy - you'll praise, finances stretched to the limit - you'll praise, body in pain - you'll praise, in need of a miracle - you'll praise, in need of a blessing - you'll praise!

Again I remind you that the Word of the Lord says that we should offer the "sacrifice" of praise to God. When you offer up a cold blooded praise, it's all sacrifice. What takes a praise from simply being a praise to being a cold-blooded praise are harsh circumstances and/or awkward timing in which the individual makes a conscious decision to offer praise to the Lord. I believe that Paul and Silas again showed us something by being able to overlook the fact that they'd been jailed and had committed no crime. They were locked up with hardened criminals and yet in the midst of their harsh circumstance and awkward timing, they made a conscious decision to sacrifice praise to God.

Many of you reading this book right now are going through the battle of your life. The pressure is on and it is literally do-or-die, but I challenge you right now where you are to lose yourself in a cold blooded praise. I dare you to adopt the mindset of the killer and with this praise assassinate the plans that the enemy has for your life and your family. I dare you to woo Him (God) to the point that He has to stop what He's doing and move on your behalf right now! Invite the Lord to leave the comfort of His throne and take a seat in the midst of your praise. Bring Him to where you are, knowing that when He shows up, He's not coming alone but He's bringing liberty with him. Lose your mind in praise and know that where liberty is, bondage cannot exist. It's all within your grasp! So right now, right where you are, put the book down, open your mouth, PRAISE YOUR GOD AND GET FREE!

PRAISE FOR PROTECTION

The Bible tells us to resist the devil and he will flee from you. Praise builds a wall of resistance against your enemies. Continue to praise and eventually you will build up a resistance that even the devil will have to acknowledge and cause him to flee from you. Why? Because the word will be out ... that the crazy praiser is at it again!

Praise doesn't just build walls of protection but praise will cause your God, the Lord of Host, He who will fight for you, to get riled up and go to war on your behalf. Let it be known that God loves a good fight and is looking for an opportunity to run to your rescue in times of trouble just as He did for Jehosaphat and the Israelites or more specifically Jehosophat and the congregations of Jerusalem and Judah or PRAISE.

And when he had consulted with the people, he appointed singers unto the Lord, and that should praise the beauty of holiness, AS THEY WENT OUT BEFORE THE ARMY, and to say Praise the Lord for his mercy endureth forever. AND WHEN THEY BEGAN TO PRAISE, THE LORD SET OUT AMBUSHMENTS AGAINST THE CHILDREN OF AMMON, MOAB AND MOUNT SEIR WHICH WERE COME AGAINST JUDAH (PRAISE) AND THEY WERE SMITTEN. (2CHRON 20:21, 22)

There are three major points that come from just these two verses of scripture.

Point one - **SEND JUDAH FIRST.** The 21st verse tells us that they (JUDAH/PRAISE) went out BEFORE the army. Jehosophat knew that no matter what was to happen IN the battle that they could win if they praised God BEFORE the battle. Send your praise before you to do what you cannot do. You may say, "that works spiritually, but how can that help me naturally in everyday life?" Your praise can go before you and change atmospheres and conditions before you get where you are going. I have heard numerous testimonies of individuals who needed the Lord to work a miracle for them in the area of credit and finances. Most of them admit that through carelessness, frivolousness and lack of wisdom, they brought on themselves negative situations, however, they still needed the Lord to move on their behalf and deliver them from this self-inflicted stronghold. Thank God for Grace! Every one of them sought the Lord on how to deal with their situations and then began to praise and magnify God in advance for their deliverance. They sent JUDAH first - for what they knew he would do for them. The result was that God spoke and gave them a plan of how to work, save and pay off their bills. He changed the condition or atmosphere of their minds. This while developing temperance in them and teaching them how to use discipline and wisdom with their finances so they wouldn't find themselves in need of this same deliverance two years down the road. The Bible tells us that if we will be faithful over a few things, God will make us ruler over many. He must first know that you can be trusted with the little He gives you before bountiful blessings can arise in our lives so we must show Him that we can be good stewards over the things He places in our lives even in the time of need.

Some had debt reductions or debt cancellation through pardons by their creditors. Their praise went before them to condition the mind of their creditors and change the atmosphere before they could make the call to work it out. Still others were the recipients of true miracles! Computer glitches began taking place in the systems of their creditors, where one day the debt was there and owed, and the next day no one could find it. I like to call these grace gifts and supernatural surprises. Although God sent deliverance to each individual in a different way, there was one common thing that took place in every situation. Before beginning to attack the financial challenges in their lives, they started praising God in advance for what they knew He would do for each of them.

Whether a natural or spiritual battle, your praise CAN get into places that you physically cannot get into and condition atmospheres before you have to walk into them.

Praise Principle: YOU ARE GOING TO HAVE TO WORK FOR THIS ONE. Those of you who are just learning and accepting this, it is not too late for you to operate in this realm of spiritual power and authority. You need only to begin and be diligent. You must know that it will not be easy because a key to mastering the art of praise is learning to push past your flesh and your emotions and just do it. This is easier said than done but can be accomplished. Mainly because this task is not one that God is going to do for you, neither will He help you by granting a miracle to make it easier. The difference between you and the praiser is that when you want something from God you pray, you cry, you beg and weep. "God please help me, I need Your help, I can't go on like this if You don't help me, I don't know what I'm gonna do". The praiser, in the same predicament, says, "Father, I bless You, I glory in You and I honor You. I thank You Lord that even in the midst of adversity I know that You are in control. I appreciate You God and I thank You because I know that no weapon formed against me will ever prosper, my life is in Your hands. You are worthy of all praise, Lord. I thank You in advance for my deliverance. Thank You for making me an over-comer. There's none like You, God. Thank you for loving me, thank You for never leaving me, thank You for the victory!" Can you see the difference? Try it and you will feel the difference as well, even at the time that you release your praise. If you really want this level of praise, you are going to have to take control of your flesh and fight for it. It is worth it. Overcoming you so you can graduate to the next level in praise means possessing the ability to forget about yourself, concentrate on Him and praise! Remember this: you cannot send Judah first if Judah isn't already with you waiting to be sent!

Those of you that have lived your life as a praiser and are already empowered in this way, there is good news for you. Praise is already part of your atmosphere. It walks with you. It's all around you because this is who you are and not just what you do. You are the ones who, at any time during your day (good or bad), the words "thank you Jesus" can slip through your lips. For you it's not about getting in gear but because you live in this realm you need only to shift to a higher gear. All you need to do is give your praise an assignment, tell it where to go and then send it to accomplish the task you've given it. SEND JUDAH FIRST!

Point two - **PRAISE IS YOUR WEAPON!**
For the weapons of our warfare are not carnal but mighty through God to the pulling down of strongholds.
II CORINTHIANS 10:4

This means no knives, no blades, no guns, no baseball bats and lead pipes! If people get on your nerves YOU CANNOT CUT THEM! I know you want to. And believe me, I know sometimes people will try and take you there because sometimes I want to. Okay, let's keep it real - a lot of times I want to! Many times people will try to take you there - especially when you have made up in your mind that you are going to do it God's way. They will take your kindness for weakness and assume now that you are saved they can treat you any way they want to because you can't retaliate. Oh no! Because saved people don't act like that! So people will push you right to the edge and then try to make you lose your balance and go over the cliff! The devil is a liar! I've got news for you and with it you can serve notice on your enemy. You still fight - you have only changed the type of weapons you use. YOUR PRAISE IS A WEAPON! It has the ability to move in and out of places you cannot go! It confuses your enemy and will disorient them to the point that they end up falling in the very grave that they dug for your burial.

So am I saying that your retaliation is your praise not only when Satan attacks but when people attack as well? YES I AM! Am I crazy? NO I AM NOT! I am not saying that if someone comes after you swinging a baseball bat at your head, that you stand there speaking in tongues waiting to see how many stitches will be required to close your sanctified and super-deep scalp. That's not what I'm saying at all. If someone comes at you that way common sense says the first thing you do is duck or get out of the way! What you do after they miss your head is between you, them and Jesus and I'm gonna pray for you. As a matter of fact, ya'll pray for me on that one, okay?

What I am saying is that people will attack your position, they will try to assassinate your character and if you are anything like me, even remotely, you want to go and let them have it! You want to defend yourself and that's only natural. You want to let them know quite frankly that although you don't fight doesn't mean you can't! Whew … I felt that one right there. Ya'll are still praying for me, right? (Smile)

But seriously, I can speak on this because I have had to learn it and live it. I am living knee-deep in it right now as I write this book.

Truthfully, anyone who really knows me knows that I am NOT a punk! But the Lord has patiently, graciously and lovingly taught me that I didn't always have to - or even need to - fight my own battles. At times this was and (I admit) still is very hard for me because again, I AM NOT a punk and something inside of me really needs to make sure that this is understood by those who would purposely and without cause seek to do me harm. But God is faithful and He says to me and you during these times just as He said to the children of Israel "be not afraid or dismayed for the battle is not yours, but God's". (II Chronicles 20:15 latter portion).

I DO THANK GOD FOR WALKING IN MY DELIVERANCE!

And you need to thank God for walking in your deliverance too!

Because the good news is that this is not just for me but it is available to all who serve the Lord. I challenge you to move to that next level of praise.

Your sacrifice of praise entitles you to more than the status quo, more than just getting by and more than just passively accepting that you have to accept whatever the enemy throws at you and smile.

I DON'T THINK SO!

So the next time you find yourself facing a battle before anything moves or happens you need to stop and take a praise break.

All He (God) wants is your praise. Praise is His incentive, His motivator, His energy drink, if you will. Praise gets God going and the more you praise the more He wants to fight for you.

PRAISE IS MY WEAPON! PRAISE IS YOUR WEAPON!

The Lord gave me a vision of just how powerful a weapon our praise can be in times of battle. I saw a big black cannon like the ones used in the wars of times past. There was, in the distance, an approaching enemy, an army. This cannon was simply moved into position in front of the enemy. It was grand and it had a presence. It was an impending threat and a constant reminder to the enemy whenever he came within eyeshot that this thing could be fired off at anytime and destroy them. There were no people around it, just the cannon. The enemy would come into view and then retreat, come into view and then retreat - each time getting a little closer than the last time. Finally, because there was no one else around that this army could see, they decided that this cannon was a dud. It had the look of a powerful weapon but it had no power. With that, the army charged forward and attempted to take the land that this cannon was set out to protect. Little did this army know that the cannon was fully loaded and ready to move into battle and fire. The enemy, unaware of the true power of this seemingly silent and harmless figure of protection, began to charge forward. Out of nowhere, came fire to the wick of the cannon to ignite it. As the cannon began to fire its ammunition, it destroyed everything that opposed it.

The revelation is this. Praise is the cannon and if praise is who you are and not just what you do, YOU are the cannon. You are a constant presence for your enemy(ies) to see. Being in that constant state of praise will keep many attacks of the enemy at bay, but for the bold enemy who would dare to walk into your land, your territory, your home, your business, your finances, your health or your life and try to posses it. Then, your shift from praise to cold-blooded praise is what brings the fire of God to ignite you - the cannon - to fire your ammunition which is the praise of warfare and destroy everything that would oppose you!

Yes, praise sets the tone before the battle. And praise is the weapon that will fight for you and lead you to victory! When in battle, the continuing sound of your praise will be the thing to make your enemy lose focus of his mission to destroy you. Recently, I sat in a service and heard the preacher give one of the most powerful revelations concerning the enemy's response to praise that I'd ever heard. I began to really think about what the preacher said and apply it to my own personal storms and challenges and the discomforts and hell that seemed to be breaking forth in my own life during that time. As I began to seek God for how this Word applied to me, He began to show me what was happening to me in the spirit realm and this is what I saw: *(I have purposely externalized this so you can more easily apply it to what you may be experiencing right now in your life)*

Imagine the devil moving full speed ahead in an attack on your life. (Some of you don't have to imagine because you are in the midst of an attack right now). Now see Satan going for your throat to try and choke the life out of you with bills, trials, confusion, marital problems or sickness. You see it coming, it's all around or it's already in full swing but you find the strength to move yourself into praise. It's not easy because he's choking you, but you put all that you are and everything that you have into making sure that the devil, his imps or even those around you who mean you no good, know that you are on a cold blooded murderous mission to kill the plan of your enemies with this praise. You begin to change your atmosphere with this praise. What your enemies set up as an intrusion for you now sounds like confusion to them. But you aren't confused, only your enemy! Your enemy is confused because he doesn't understand how you can praise when he's hitting you with his best shots. He tightens the grip to make you stop praising, only you praise even harder and now the enemy is beginning to become annoyed. He doesn't like the sound of your praise. It aggravates him. It gets on his nerves. It makes him sick. You praise even stronger. The enemy is becoming increasingly agitated and fidgety and looking for a way to block the sound from his ears because he doesn't want to hear your praise. You begin to experience extreme discomfort. It seems like this discomfort is the most you've felt throughout this entire tribulation. This discomfort is not because you are losing ground, but this period of extreme discomfort you feel is because the devil's hands are still around your throat and now he is squirming and trying to figure out a way to get his ears covered to block the sound of your voice. He's looking for help from his homies, the imps, but they won't come to cover him because they can't get that close to the sound of this praise because they are weaker than he is and if he can't take it they surely can't take it. All this movement and struggle from Satan in the spiritual realm is making things look and feel a lot worse than they are in the natural realm. To you, it feels like the hold is getting stronger and it's getting harder to breathe because his hands are around your throat and he won't stop squirming. In life this is the time when everything looks as if its about to crash and burn all around you, yet this is also the time when every word of prophecy or encouragement that comes to you says not to give up, hold on, that you are right at the point of your breakthrough and your miracle is getting ready to manifest in your life. It almost doesn't make sense that this is the greatest discomfort you've had, yet you are hearing that you are right at the point of your breakthrough. It's getting so hard at this point that if you ever saw your breakthrough in the distance you can't see it anymore, if you'd ever felt like it was going to get better it certainly doesn't feel like it now and everything around you is looking dim. You're weary but you're still praising and just when you feel like you are going out for the count, the Lord blows a wind into your spirit and gives you what you need to go this last round. A shift comes into your spirit and you find yourself moving from praise to cold-blooded praise. Your attitude is do-or-die! You have nothing to lose and you GO FOR WHAT YOU KNOW! The look in your eyes intensifies, your countenance changes and all you see is red. Red because something clicks in your mind and you remember that you are covered by the blood of Jesus and then red again for that cold-blooded praise mode that the thought of Jesus' blood has just propelled you to. Your mission is to kill the plan of the enemy. You are now praising like you have lost your mind! Your whole body is involved in this praise. Now the enemy's grip on your neck is beginning to loosen because he cannot take it. Now, instead of the position of the choke-hold, Satan is positioning himself to cover his ears to block the sound of your praise and as he is removing his hands from your throat, as he is loosing you - as he is letting you go, as he is freeing you from his grip so follows the freeing of your health, your marriage, your children, your finances, your body, your mind, your spirit. YOU ARE FREE!

Isn't that an awesome revelation? Our God is an awesome God! You ought to put the book down and right where you are, give God cold-blooded praise because of the Word you just received to help you make it through the end of this trial. Come on - close your eyes. Now picture the devil standing in front of you with his hands covering his ears with a look of absolute terror just before he takes off and runs from you - releasing you and all your stuff!

NOW OPEN YOUR MOUTH, FORGET WHERE YOU ARE, FORGET WHO'S AROUND YOU AND PRAISE!

You ought to feel victory in your soul at this moment. And depending on how far you let yourself go on that one, a little time may have passed since you put the book down. But read on, I got you covered, you can start right where you left off - unless you want to backtrack and start your personal praise party all over again. You can do that too. The book will be here when you and the Lord get finished.

Point Three - VICTORY IS GUARANTEED TO YOU (THE PRAISER). Now you understand that in every battle, to guarantee victory, your praise must go first. Now you have learned that your praise should already be an established part of your life so that you are authorized to send it before you move into battle. Now you realize that the weapon of praise is all you need - not the weapons of our mouth, the weapons of our connections (who we know) or the weapons of the phone call we can make to get back at our enemies. And definitely not guns, knives or a fist need to go before you in battle because we know the weapons of our warfare are not carnal. Right now all you need to concentrate on is looking down the road, seeing yourself victorious and as you walk in the direction of your complete deliverance, walk with the understanding that victory is guaranteed to you because you are a praiser.

Chapter Seventeen
THE DICTATION OF PRAISE

There is a little exercise that I'd like to teach you called the *Dictation of Praise*. I don't mean dictation as it relates to dictatorship or harsh and cruel leadership of one individual over many. No, that's not what this means. This is dictation as in "grab a pen and paper and take this dictation." It sounds strange I'm sure, but it will all make sense in a few minutes. Think about it now. If you could tailor what your motions of praise said to God more in depth than what the words of your mouth say when you praise, how would you do it? What would you say? What would you want your motion of praise or your body language to mean if it were interpreted with the words of your choosing?

Many people are not good at speaking words or clever phrases. Some will never be great orators or speech makers. Most will never be great worship leaders whose job is to lead the masses into the act of praise and worship. But that's alright because remember, praise comes from your private places, which means that praise is never about quantity as it relates to eloquence and verbal skills, but it is always about quality - the purity and sincerity of your praise. I encourage you to try this personal praise exercise at home or some other private haven and do it often. Although great praise can and does come forth in more official settings, this is designed primarily for your personal one-on-one time with the Lord. And remember, some of your most liberating praise experiences will take place not in a church service with hundreds or thousands of people around, but in a private place such as your home or your car anyway.

Step one - Make an appointment and keep it.
Many times we set prayer and or devotion times and we don't keep them. I have been guilty of that myself in the past. We get busy, something comes up and we push it off or we say "I'll do it later or next time." What many of us do that's even worse is we totally forget that we ever made the appointment to begin with! Why is it that we show our clients, our bosses, our colleagues, friends and even our doctors more respect for their time than we do God? When we plan to meet for lunch, to go shopping or if we have a doctor's appointment not only do we show up and on time, but many times we get there early. And we dare not be late or miss the doctor's appointment especially since it is possible that the charge for the visit could be enforced even if you are not seen! As such, we seem to respect man's time more than God's time and this is unacceptable. In God you live, move and have your being. If not for Him you would be nothing that you are (even if you are not crazy about who you are) and would never be who you will be, yet we take Him for granted in this manner. We as Christians must right this wrong and this will help you to do that. This part of the exercise is to help you develop discipline when it comes to keeping your devotion time with the Father, so keep your appointment!

Step Two - Get a paper and pen.
You have just become your own spiritual secretary. You may have done this in times past and not really understood what you were doing or how significant it was. By writing down words of prophecies spoken over your life, or dreams and visions that you have had or even the more commonly known prayer list that many of us keep, you were taking spiritual or Heavenly dictation.

Step Three - Sit, think and itemize.
Now you must begin to think about a few things that you really want to show God some appreciation for. The length of your list is really up to you, but I would say don't make the list too long. I believe you can really put out a higher grade of praise to God when you are concentrating on one or two (but not more than a few) things. Each time you do this exercise you will

have a new Dictation of Praise for that appointment and, as such, it is not necessary to try to remember everything you can remember from your childhood in this one instance. Besides, if this works out the way it is designed to, this praise exercise will be something that will become quite addictive and you will do it often, giving yourself many opportunities to thank God for many things. Now if you are feeling like you just want to go all out and have a Dictation of Praise marathon than go for it. This will usually be ideal if you are on consecration, shutting in. Write a healthy list and prepare to spend some quality time with the Lord for this appointment. God is definitely worth and worthy of the time.

Step Four - Begin your dictation.
***Note: This exercise is going to be done in letter format so place the date on it, and - if you are feeling extra creative - put a heavenly address on it. There's no need to feel silly or embarrassed. No one will ever see this but you.

Write your letter to God and, using your list from step three, tell Him what it is you want to thank Him for. Now that you have told Him what you want to thank Him for, tell Him why. It doesn't matter if your grammar is correct, if the sentence structure is accurate or the expressions you use makes sense.

This is just you and the Lord. He already knows what's in your heart, He just wants you to bring it to Him. He can interpret your broken English, split verbs, slang terminology and Ebonics all day long and why wouldn't He be able to? If he can interpret our groans when we cry to him; if He understood the cries of injustice from the blood of Abel when his brother Cain brutally murdered him, what makes you think He doesn't understand your improper English or grammar?

God doesn't care about any of that because this praise is coming from your private place and being transported from the eternal parts of your soul into the established place in time for your secret rendezvous with Him!

Say all you want to say in this letter, get as creative and as expressive as you want. Be daring - go out on a limb and use words that you might not dare attempt when speaking to people, for fear of their improper use. This is not about anything other than the fact that you recognize, "hey it's just me and my Father and I don't mind looking foolish in front of Him. He will honor it."

Finish your letter and sign it.

Step Five - Read your Dictation.
When you have finished your letter, sit up and read it aloud with great enthusiasm as if the Lord was right there in the room with you, seated in front of you, giving you His undivided attention. Again, don't think of this as foolish. Do not allow thoughts to come to your mind and tell you that this is crazy or silly. Read your letter and know that the Lord will honor this commitment you've made and meet you there every time. And you will know He's there because as you begin to take yourself (your mind) out of that room and put yourself into this praise, you will feel Him right there with you. Some of you will even begin to hear Him talk to you!

Step Six - Go crazy with praise ... excluding no part of your body!
Now that you have made your appointment and kept it, got your tools and prepared (paper and pen), thought about the things you want to praise God for and itemized them and then written your letter and read it to the Lord, it's time to get this party started! You have already told the Lord everything you wanted Him to know about this praise that you are getting ready to give. So if you never get around to calling it out you have already labeled and interpreted what your body and purpose is praising for even if you become so spiritually inebriated that you cannot verbalize it in your native language.

That is it! It's that simple. Six easy steps to opening a whole new way for you to give God praise and show Him you really appreciate Him.

A lot of you may be thinking, "Well that sounds good but I've never heard of that before. I don't know if it makes sense." Well, first you really have heard of this before. This is really no different than having a prayer list that you use to keep up with all the things and people that you don't want to forget to pray for. The one major difference between this letter and your prayer list is that you will not ask God for one thing during this time of personal devotion. This time is set aside just to make God feel special for all that He is, all that He's done, all that He's promised to do and for just being God. So rather than calling this a prayer list you can call it a praise list. Because of the format in which I have you write it, I call it the *Dictation of Praise*. So what are you waiting on? Set an appointment with God to write Him His letter and read it to Him and then praise Him! Remember this is a priority, and part of this exercise is disciplining yourself to respect God the way you would a client or your boss or some other person with whom you would have to make an appointment to see.

I want you to try this. Make up in your mind today that you are going to do it just once and see what happens. I believe that you will never view personal praise time the same way again and I know you will see results like none other.

Some of you may still be unsure, even with the steps laid out, of how to put it all together. I feel that this praise method is so powerful and will bring such great results to your walk that I don't want anyone to be left out, so I have put together a mock Dictation of Praise that I have taken from King David's praise dance that concluded with him naked in the middle of the courtyard.

DAVID'S DICTATION OF PRAISE

Oh God My Father,
I love You so much. I thank You for all that You are and everything You do. Lord I honor You for being most holy, most righteous, the sovereign God. I thank You that You looked on me one day and decided that I, who the world, even my own family, saw as nothing, as useless and nothing more than common kid who would never do more than clean up after sheep, in me You saw greatness. In me You saw a king! I praise You because before I ever had a clue of who I was to be while I was yet tending sheep You had me in preparation for the life that would surely be mine. You anointed me as a child to kill ferocious animals because You knew I'd have to kill Goliath and I say thank You Lord. I thank You that in spite of everything, even my brothers who should've come before me for any greatness out of my Father's house You chose me. You have taken me through wars and made me victorious. You have delivered me from the hand of King Saul who once admonished me before the people, even gave me his daughter for a wife, eventually turned and sought to kill me. You continue to deliver me from enemies that rise against me and Your people. You comfort me even though my wife who has the same spirit as her father Saul would scoff and mock me as I praise You. You spoke a word over my life at a young age that I would be King and in spite of every attempt by my adversary to kill me before I reached that destiny You kept me and fulfilled your Word. And now for this I thank You. With my mouth I thank You. With my heart I lift You up. With my soul I give You glory and with my whole body I give You praise! There is none like You Lord. I honor You now. There is no part of me that is too good to lose control over for Your glory. These clothes that I wear are expensive and beautiful but if they must tear let them tear! I have none of this except You give it to

me and I am nothing that I am except You make me who I am. God I know I'm the King, I know there are protocols and I know that I'm being watched but I don't care what anybody else thinks. This is about me and You and how much I love You and how much I adore You and how much I appreciate You and I need to let You know it right now! So let me be a fool for You, let my wife mock me, let the handmaidens watch if they will, let me drain my body of all its energy in an effort to show You how I feel. Nothing else matters and no one else matters.

This is from my heart. Please accept it as I give it. Because I really love You.

Your Son,
David, The Shepherd

And David danced before the Lord with all his might; and David was girded with a linen ephod (2 SAMUEL 6:14)

Chapter Eighteen
YOUR SON, DAVID, THE SHEPHERD

There are two things I'd like to point out to you and expound on just a little.

The letter and its contents are self explanatory so I won't go any further there. I do want to point out the closing of the letter and the scripture that follows it here in the book from which God inspired and spoke to me the revelation of David's Dictation of Praise.

YOUR SON, DAVID, THE SHEPHERD.

Your son, David -- this is a clear acknowledgment on the part of David to the special relationship he has with the Father. Possibly even a little bit of a reminder to God so that when his praises go up before the throne, God would say, yes, that praise has the odor of my son on it. Sometimes when children get past the 18-year mark, they will do something they know is in complete contradiction to their upbringing because they think they are grown and don't have to do what Mama or Daddy says any longer. The result is they have to be reminded sharply that no matter how grown they think they are or will be, they will always be the child in the parent/child relationship and must respect that. David didn't have that problem. He wanted God to know, "King or no King, I am Your boy! Just call me Junior!" When the time would come that God would have to punish David, He would remember, see and hear the praise David offered but He would smell the odor and say, "that's my son." It was important to him that he remained in God's eyes as His favored child, so he acknowledged the relationship always.

And, ladies and gentlemen, without a doubt, he certainly did acknowledge that - even when he was completely out of line.

The Shepherd - Now by this time in David's life we all know he was King. Not only was he the king but his reputation as a great man of war went before him. So why would he take down and refer to himself as a lowly shepherd boy? Because in David's private place of praise, that's who he was. No matter what elevations David reached, no matter how his riches increased or how many nations and kingdoms he conquered, David always kept a place where he could return to the purity and simplicity of the times when no one else was around or even cared to be. Those were the times when, as a kid, everyone said he was nothing and full of folly. Those were the days before life became too filled with other obligations and it was just him and God communing for hours and hours day after day. The shepherd represents him coming to Christ as a child the way the Word tells us we must do. David was competitive. This was evident from early on his life by the way he took on slaying wild animals, the way he took on Goliath and even later in life, the way he waged and fought wars against his enemies and, yes, even in the way he pursued another man's wife. David did not like failure - it wasn't an option. But as important as winning was to David, God's opinion of him was always more important. David praised because he knew that was the way to let God know what was in his heart. So in coming to the Father as the shepherd, although he was king, he took himself back to a place where out of his mouth had to come perfected praise because this praise came from the heart of a babe. The babe that lived in the private place of King David, God's son, the shepherd.

And David danced before the Lord with all his might:
And David was girded with a linen ephod
(II SAMUEL 6:14)

And David danced before the Lord with ALL his might - here again is an example of David's second nature kicking in and him losing himself in praise. This example of praise is the infamous praise dance we hear so much about in church where David danced so hard before the Lord that he actually came out of his clothes! We always hear that David was also a man after God's own heart. This simply means that David was God's beloved, somewhat of a favorite child or "teacher's pet," if you will. David learned how to praise and worship the Father in any circumstance. He even worshipped when he was in the wrong because it was a part of who he was. But it was David's praise and worship that kept him pure. So even when David was wrong, God could get a message to him - "I love you son, but you are wrong and you need to straighten up." The interesting thing about this instance in which David praised God is that he had just come through a time (while transporting the ark*) where he knew he'd been displeasing to the Father. This dance was in conjunction with the ceremonial events and sacrifices connected to the transporting of the ark, however, I believe because of David's error in judgment and his need to make it right during this time, he kicked it up several notches! David's demeanor was like that of a child who could not bear the thought of having Daddy upset with him so he always set out to stay in the good graces of God. That was the motivation behind this praise that went forth from David. He wanted to let God know he was repentant and that there was nothing and no one that meant so much to him. David was even ridiculed by his wife because she felt that by dancing out of his clothes he'd behaved himself in a manner that was beneath the way a king and priest should carry himself. She really lit into David (the way an unwise loose-lipped woman can) and berated him. However David let her know he didn't care. He felt that when it came to giving God glory it took all of that and then some. He let her know that when he praises, if he sees that he can go further, he will without hesitation. In this, David set the standard for high praise and clearly he did because it is the most talked-about instance of David's displays of praise even though he lived his entire life as a praiser.

And David was girded with a linen ephod - I love this part of the scripture. It is mentioned rather passively and not with much emphasis but it grabbed my attention because it made me think of the way Jabez and the prayer he prayed was mentioned in the Bible (I CHRONICLES 4: 9-10). The mention of Jabez and his now very popular prayer for his coasts or borders to be enlarged, was snuck in during the rundown of the genealogy of Judah. Realize now that there was something so significant about him that the writer deemed it necessary to break from his train of thought and talk to you about the faith this one man had for God to change his life and bring him increase. This is what I feel about the mention of the ephod. To make you understand we must look closer. The ephod was a garment that was worn in those days by the priest specifically for ceremonial rites. The linen ephod was a garment of distinction and symbolized the highest order of the church in those days, so it was respected. The individual who wore it was respected and sat as the top tier in the hierarchy of the church. There was dignity attached to the very presence of the ephod. To put it more plainly you might borrow someone's robe or sandals in those days. You wouldn't borrow an ephod! That would be like someone borrowing your wedding ring! No one other than the priest wore this particular garment so you knew that when you saw it you were looking at spiritual royalty. David was King, but he was also priest, so while participating in the transporting of the ark (which was a very sacred thing), he was adorned in his ephod. He was a man of distinction. No one present was more rich, more distinguished, more famous or had more notoriety than David, yet he let himself go to the point of losing all inhibitions (if he had any) and praised God to the point of no return. So what does this have to do with you? I am not telling you to strip down to your underwear the next time you dance before the Lord, (unless of course you are in your own private space and you feel like it). What I am saying is you must strip yourself of your linen ephod. And just what is your linen ephod? Your ephod is your status. Your ephod is the name you have made for yourself in society. Your ephod is your reputation or your cool and laid back demeanor. Simply put, you are not so rich, so famous, so distinguished, so cute, so beautiful or handsome, or so important that you cannot let go and give God the true and pure praise He deserves to receive from you. He's done so much for you. You owe it to Him!

DAVID PRAISED ALWAYS

Please keep in mind that in this point in David's life he had not committed what the world would know as his greatest sin (the taking of Bathsheba, having an affair with her, impregnating her and the killing of Uriah, her husband). David had not experienced the embarrassment, hurt and shame of his son Amnon raping his own sister (Tamar), nor had he yet experienced the uprising and betrayal of his beloved son Absalom who would turn the affection of the people toward himself above and away from his father, the king, for the purpose of overthrowing him from his seat of power and taking his life. However I say to you that in spite of all of the ups and downs that David experienced (some that I didn't mention and many of which he caused on himself) there was always the existence of a private place where his praise came from and dwelt. The purity of that place and the sincerity of his heart even when his flesh wouldn't do right, kept him as a favored child of the Father, even when He had to chastise him. It was because of the way David positioned himself in the heart of God through his praise that the Lord had already provided the escape routes that would bring David to restoration in the trying times he would surely face.

So if we are wise, we would learn from the best and understand that the sacrifice of time for the sacrifice of praise is more for our own benefit than anything else. There will come a time when you will need to be remembered as the favored child of God. It may very well be at the hand of a self-inflicted mess, however, wouldn't it be great to know that because you didn't allow yourself to become that adult child who was too big for his britches and didn't have to listen anymore "because I'm grown" that the Father would help you, even in the time of correction? Wouldn't it be nice to know that because you kept your praise in that private place and kept it pure that God could identify you as His child by the odor of your praise?

Do like David and remain a son. Stay humble before the Father no matter how elevated you may be in society or in the church. If you keep the heart of David, the son and the shepherd, you will always be in God's heart.

Chapter Nineteen
PRAISE COMES FROM YOUR PRIVATE PLACES

I believe many things in life. Like all of you reading this book, I have my ways about me just like you do. I am strong willed. I can be a little stubborn at times. I am good natured - but not a push-over. I believed it when the old folks said "baby, if you don't stand for something you'll fall for anything!" I truly believe that by-standing in silence when you know of wrongdoing is to be in support of it. I'm real and I can't be phony even when there is something to be gained from it.

I believe I will one day write my autobiography and have the opportunity to go deep about the events of my life, but now is not the time. I do feel that at this point in the book it is important to share a little more of who I am with you than what you already know. It is important that you understand how some of the circumstances of my life have brought me to be "sold out for God" no matter what!

MY PRIVATE PLACE

From a very young age I endured mental, emotional and physical abuse at the hands of close friends and relatives. I have had attempts made on my body at the hands of babysitters in my home and preachers, deacon and credential holders in the local church and the organization that I grew up in. The attempts were bold and brazen and one was even made right in the church during a service. I saw and heard a lot of things that no child should. I carried the secrets of many throughout my childhood and wouldn't talk because I felt the need to protect those around me. There did come a time when I did want to talk about certain things (such as one of the preacher incidents), but I was told to keep my mouth shut. Some things were better off left alone, I was told. I was 13. There was another time that while visiting a church member's house for a sleep-over with his daughters, I was taken for a drive into the middle of the woods at 5:00 a.m. and was attacked. I refused to stop fighting and because of God's grace, he could not finish what he started. I was 11.

I was a very outspoken child, a truth teller and quite blunt about it at times. Because I was raised under the old and strict Pentecostal regime, this trait was not embraced or encouraged in children, but rather deemed disrespectful. As a result, this was the reputation I earned because I would speak up when things were not right, even if it was an adult. I fought to protect myself and many times it was with words because I was good at it. I learned and came to believe at an early age that it was me against the world. And most of my lessons were taught by the saved, sanctified, Holy Ghost-filled, fire-baptized, tongue-talking Christians I went to church with. I have had a personal relationship with Jesus Christ since the age of 7. I'd prayed the prayer of faith many times before then (because they made us do it) but it was around this age that I remember really learning how to communicate with God privately and independently. I started writing songs at this age. As a child, I saw things in dreams and told people and they didn't believe me. Those things would come to pass but no one would address it so I learned to keep my dreams to myself.

I saw angels and I knew when God was getting ready to do something special. I recall sitting in a choir rehearsal late one Friday night in a church in Brooklyn, NY. The mothers of that church were in the prayer room in the upper level. Standing in the choir stand, which faced the sanctuary from its elevated position behind the pulpit, I looked up and saw seven angels enter the sanctuary in the upper balcony. They stood very orderly in a straight line facing the pulpit and choir stand and they appeared simply to be watching over the 70 or 80 choir members present. Six of them looked to be the size of an average man and one had the height of a giant. It stood at least two feet taller than the other angels. Their formation was forward-facing with three man-sized angels to the left, three man-sized angels to the right and the one giant-sized angel in the middle. It was clear to me that the one in the middle was in charge. They were all adorned in plain white garments with a robe-like appearance; however the garment of the giant angel - the archangel - was much grander and had what looked like more layers and detail to it than the others. All of their faces were non-descript. At first I thought I was seeing things since it was very late and rehearsal didn't start until after Friday night worship had ended. So I rubbed my eyes and blinked a few times but they didn't go anywhere. I kept my eyes fixed on them to see why they were there. The choir finished the song we were learning and everyone started talking and laughing. I was watching the angels because I knew something special was about to happen. The choir director began to 'shhh' the members. His mood changed very rapidly from playful to one of reverence - as if he felt their presence. He began to talk softly and I looked up. The archangel (the one in the middle) nodded his head as if to say "yes, right now" and a glory fell in that rehearsal. No more songs were sung that night. As the mothers continued their all-night prayer in the upper rooms of that sanctuary the spirit of worship overtook us and rehearsal came to an abrupt end to make way for the presence of the Lord. As choir members began worshipping in their heavenly language people began weeping and sobbing and receiving spiritual breakthroughs. I watched the angels turn and leave the same way they entered. It was a special visitation. God favored us that night. To this day I don't know if someone else in that rehearsal walked away with a tangible miracle as a result of that instance. And I really don't know why God chose me to witness what I saw. But through that experience, I got a chance, as a young child, to see how God can have you on His mind and decide "I want to come and touch my children just because." Think about that for a minute and see the contrast. Isn't it awesome that the majestic Jesus Christ wouldn't think it robbery to leave His throne in all of its splendor and glory where He is being honored and worshipped in total purity by the Cherubim and Seraphim (angels) and come to dirty, roach-filled, rat-infested Brooklyn to visit His beloved and wrap them in His glory? Come on and get spiritual with me for a minute. When is the last time He visited you right in the middle of your mess, dirt and filth just so you would know that in spite of how you'd messed things up, that he still loves you. MMMM - that's good.

Needless to say, everyone left the rehearsal that night in a state of spiritual inebriation, and to this day I have never forgotten that night.

I grew up in poverty. I have been homeless twice, both times before the age of 18. I have now - and even from my early childhood, as I just explained - had a discerning eye and spirit, especially with people. If I don't like you, you'll know it. If I do like you, you'll know that too. And if I love you, it's until death do us part. I've found that to be true not just in my marriage but in my friendships as well. There have been friendships that God has caused me to let go. I have literally had to learn to let go and still love from a distance. It's that God kind of love that makes it possible to walk away from a person, yet love their soul to life.

I have always been one who believes in protocol and in order. I believe that if there are certain rules in a house, even if it's not your way of doing things, you are subject to those rules while you are in that house. This is true both naturally and spiritually (for those of you who pick and choose the rules of your church that you follow). I believe that if you have been given specific directions to follow to complete a task, those directions should be followed through to completion as given. I agree that when you are trying to connect with people of power or authority and there is a protocol that must be kept and a chain of command that must be respected to get to that individual, without a doubt it should be respected and followed to the letter. And I believe that when you need information, understanding or clarity on anything, you go to the leading authority in that field! I believe that excellence breeds excellence. I believe that for every cause there is an effect, for every beginning there must be an end, there is a purpose to every tragedy (we as humans usually don't accept this very willingly, but it's true and I've learned that through many personal tragedies of my own), to every thing there is a season (the Bible said that long before the Beatles did!) and for every life there is a divine destiny.

There are many other beliefs that I have and I could list, but I will end with this one. I believe that praise comes from your private places. More than that, I believe it MUST come from your private places. How can anyone truly give God praise unless he has overcome some life experience that reminds him why God should be praised? So for all of you who stopped to ask what does any of this stuff from her childhood that she is talking about have to do with praise? These are some of my private places. There are so many more that I could've shared with you (you'll have to wait for my autobiographical series) but I gave you just enough to make clear my point.

Chapter Twenty
PROFILE OF A PRAISER

Praise from a private place is really the only way to touch the heart of God. So often we sit in church and the worship leader says, "Clap your hands and give God praise" or "open you mouth and give God praise." Our mood or what our physical body feels at that time will determine whether or not we truly praise at that moment. Many of us will clap our hands or speak a word associated with giving God praise as a programmed response. We know that when someone says "Praise the Lord everybody!" we respond with "Praise the Lord!" or we otherwise act out some form of praise, but with no real sincerity. This is because that praise didn't come from a private place. How many times have you sat in a testimony or devotional service (that's the old-fashioned song service) or in a praise and worship service (that's the new-fashioned song service) and just sort of went along and went through the motions of everything happening. Sometimes in a bad mood or physically you were just tired or didn't feel well and in some cases your mood was okay and so was your health but there was just no real effort to press on and go the extra mile. The song made you feel good and you clapped but not to the point of where the atmosphere of your soul changed. You didn't really praise until your spirit was quickened and had to shift gears. Think about it. This is what I call a passive praise. FYI - this kind of praise gains you NO POINTS in glory! You cannot have the attitude that you are doing God a favor when you praise Him. Although we were created to praise the Lord, please understand that God doesn't NEED you to praise Him! He does however, want us to praise Him. I will show you why in a minute. Everything in creation that was created by God praises Him in the way that was designed for them to praise the Creator.

The trees, plants, animals and even angels praise God in their own way. They do so based on their instinct or nature placed in them at the time of their creation. By instinct the animals and vegetation of the world do their jobs within the life cycle (they work) and they praise. They work and they praise, they work and they praise, THEY WORK AND THEY PRAISE! It is built into their cycle and they cannot deter from it.

Angels praise and they praise and, well, they praise, and when they are not praising they are taking assignments or jobs or work that is issued to them by YOUR praise. Whether the commission is to go and get your finances and bring them to you because of your praise or if it is to go to war for you in the spirit realm because of your praise they stay praise connected. Notice the pattern? Just in case you don't understand my point, PRAISERS ARE NOT LAZY! They work! I already told you that praise requires energy and that the very definition of energy is the capacity (position or ability) for doing work. So, if you are not active in Kingdom building or in your local assembly which is Kingdom building, please don't call yourself a praiser and insult the rest of us who truly are. You don't fit the profile and by reason of that you are lazy! So my advice to you is to get active and then reapply for the position!

I told you before that there are two things that make praise from us (humans/mankind) special or different in the sight of God (as it compares to everything else in creation).

The first is that because He has given us free will, unlike any other of His creations, our praise to Him represents a sacrifice or a bending of our will. We don't have to praise Him, it really is a choice. But it is a choice He gave us. So when we make time, bend our will or step out of our flesh to praise God, He takes it personally because by virtue of free will which He gave us, we don't have to. My question is - why wouldn't you want to?

The second thing that really makes our praise special to God is His emotional connection to us. God is connected to us in a way that He isn't connected to anything else in creation. This hits closer to our understanding of God with us as emotional beings. God - just like you - wants to feel appreciated when He does things for those He loves. Many of you are saying she's crazy - God is above all of that emotional stuff and He doesn't need to be validated by us because He's God! God doesn't need validation from us, this is true. He is God and He's sovereign. He does however, WANT US TO WANT TO love, appreciate and validate with purity of heart the things that He does for us. You still don't believe me? Go back with me in your Bible to the book of Genesis where we are told that man was created in God's image. It is agreeable that we are shapen in the image of God.

The relationship of Father to child is fashioned after the relationship of God to man. The emotions that are inside of all of us came from God. They are all necessary to make us whole and complete people capable of living through any life situation. I'll prove that too. This is why the Bible tells us to be angry and sin not. That is because anger is an emotion that God has and has felt at many recorded times through history. We got that emotion from Him as well and because He placed it in us He knew there would be times that it would rise. So instead of leaving to chance the way we would handle our anger when it does rise, He gave us specific instructions on how to be angry and not sin. Acknowledge what has made you upset but don't act while in that emotion. So if the emotion of anger in us comes from God - who created us in His likeness - then why not the desire to feel appreciated?

A SIMPLE THANK YOU WILL DO

When parents do things for their children they do them because they love them and want the best for them. When you do things for family members and friends you do them because you love them and want the best for them. When you have made up your mind to do something for someone, there's nothing that will turn you away from that. You do it because you want to and never expect anything in return (most of us do, the rest of ya'll I'm praying for you!), but it still makes you feel so good when someone comes back to you and says "thank you." They are two little words but they carry a lot of weight. This is just like God when He decides to bless us, only He's looking out for the whole world and not just you in your corner of it. How must God feel that although He keeps our bodies functioning to capacity while we sleep at night so it doesn't shut down and send us into eternity, that we don't remember that it's Him? Most of the humans in the world do this everyday. How must He feel that although He gives us breath every morning, so we can hear the alarm clock, and go on with our days, that we don't have enough time to kneel and pray before we go to work, school or elsewhere? Most of the humans in the world do this everyday. How would you feel? Would you continue to move on behalf of millions, perhaps billions, of ungrateful people? Yet He is faithful and He has already decided that every morning He is going to breathe life and extend mercy and grace for another day and nothing stops Him from doing it. Even YOU with your semi-grateful, I-don't-have-time, sorry-excuse-giving self! You think the feeling of appreciation from you doesn't gratify God's emotion toward you? What happened in the New Testament when Jesus healed the ten lepers and told them go show themselves to the priest? They all took off because they were glad to be healed, but one remembered and came back to tell Jesus thank you. Jesus asked him where the other nine were. Their healing was something that was going to happen simply because the Lord had already made up His mind about healing those lepers. And when only one returned, He didn't unheal the other nine. He was moved at the thoughtfulness of the one who returned, but disappointed that the others did not make time to appreciate what He'd done.

This is what separates you from everything else in creation. This is what makes you special. This is what makes your praise to God mean more than any of the praise from any other creature. You have free will and God is connected to you emotionally. This is why we must stay praise connected so that we can stay connected to Him. This takes me back to what I call a *passive praise*. If you are giving God a passive praise, I have a newsflash for you - you really aren't praising Him at all. You are wasting His time and the borrowed breath that He loaned you to be here. You must tap into your private place in order to really give God a praise that He deserves and a praise that counts. For me, that is to dig into the place of my hurt, my secrets and my memories and think of how the Devil meant for the tragedies in my life to be the end of me but God used it for the building up of me and I am standing today. For you, it is the same. You must dig into your private place - the place of your wounds, your hurts, your disappointments. These are the inner crevasses of your soul. The praise that comes from this place is unparalleled and it touches the very heart of God. What happens eventually is that this private place that houses your fears and wounds and hurts becomes the place where you store your praise so even when you have been healed, this is where that powerful praise comes from. It changes from the place that once stored your hurts and all your negative emotions and dirty little secrets to the place that holds the secret of your success!

SECTION IV
The Abundant Life

Chapter Twenty-One
THE QUALIFICATIONS FOR TOTAL LIFE PROSPERITY

All our lives, we've been taught that God desires that we, His children, prosper and be in health even as our souls prosper. The problem is that while most Christians have become masters at quoting scriptures, they either don't attempt to live them or they don't really believe them. Either way it is a tragedy because I've got revelation for those in particular. If you take the time to dissect that verse of scripture you'll understand why your life seems like it just won't get better.

Beloved (my dear one) I wish above all things (my greatest desire) that you prosper (is that you receive wealth) and be in health (and your bodies be whole) even as thy soul prospereth (this in accordance and equally to the way your soul and spirit matures, grows and elevates in the Lord)
3 JOHN 1:2

NEWSFLASH! ACCORDING TO THIS - MANY OF US DON'T QUALIFY.

I know many of you don't like the sound of that, but it's true. Based on the way that verse of scripture reads, that desire is projected only to those who take the time to seek the Lord diligently for spiritual growth, promotion and power. These are the ones who do more than sit satisfied with knowing that they are forgiven Christians waiting to get to Heaven but they actively seek new heights in Christ. The initial result manifests itself as an outpouring in the spirit. The more the individual seeks the Lord that outpouring turns into an overflow and the overflow moves from the things in the spirit, into natural life causing everything about them - or even connected to them - to become saturated with the anointing and with divine promotion. The end result is prosperity to your soul and to your life.

BUT SEEK YE FIRST THE KINGDOM OF GOD, AND HIS RIGHTEOUSNESS; AND ALL THESE THINGS SHALL BE ADDED UNTO YOU.
MATT 6:33

So believe that God desires not just for us to be saved from sin but to be delivered into a life of personal fulfillment and prosperity as well.

Now, having said all of that, please know that the fact still remains that everyone around you will not experience this type of glorious living in their salvation. This does not mean they are not saved and are not going to Heaven. What it does mean is that they are most definitely living beneath their privilege as children of God have allowed themselves to be satisfied with the bare minimum that salvation has to offer. They believe that Jesus is the son of God that He died and rose for their sins, that one day He is coming back to rapture His church and that they can now go to Heaven because they believe. They got saved simply to miss Hell and go to Heaven. Their entire state of mind is that they must be saved so that when they die they can go to Heaven, thereby making them a slave to the "rules of salvation" and the role of the Christian (which in most cases are rules of religion and are man-made and not Biblical) making it virtually impossible for the individual to enjoy the beauty of relationship and walking hand in hand with the Savior along the way.

But for those of you who would stretch beyond the minimum, dig a little deeper and reach a little higher - to you comes the revelation of *beloved I would that you would prosper and be in health even as your soul prospers*. For you,

Heaven is the final destination on a flight that has been filled with wonderful layovers! You believe that God desires happiness for you in EVERY AREA of your life. You don't accept that you have to be poor. You don't accept that you have to be sick. You believe that your marriage should be the envy of all who know you and your spouse. You will not accept that your children shouldn't be well-adjusted, at the head of their class, non-drinking, non-smoking, non-experimenting, non-addicted, non-fornicating young people who love the Lord and will serve Him boldly and without shame even in their youth. You refuse to believe that you must be downtrodden in the name of Jesus. You have received the revelation that God did not save you so you would be ready to die, but He saved you so you would be equipped to live!

That was good - and I'm gonna retype it boldly for all of you whose theology just got shaken.

GOD DID NOT SAVE YOU SO YOU WOULD BE READY TO DIE, BUT HE SAVED YOU SO YOU WOULD BE EQUIPPED TO LIVE!

Chapter Twenty-Two
THE PARABLE OF THE AMUSEMENT PARK

I am very excited about this chapter. In it I am using a story-telling technique as old as the writings of the Bible itself.

Some of you are flipping through your Bibles saying, "I missed that one. What book is the parable of the amusement park in?" Maybe if I check the index…?" Still others of you are saying, "she's crazy! I told you that singer girl doesn't have any Word in her, I knew I was right!"

Before you get too far out there on your tangent, let me reel you back in. There is no parable of the amusement park in the Bible. I didn't say it was in the Bible. I am well aware that it is not. This is just another way the Lord has given me to put into extremely simple terms the experience of salvation to help dispel the myths long believed by the world that receiving Christ and accepting salvation means being super broke all the time, super serious all the time and super happy none of the time.

Jesus used parables all the time so that the people would understand Him when He needed to get a point across. If it worked for Him I figure it can work for me. AMEN AND SELAH!

Let's take a closer look shall we?

THE PARABLE OF THE AMUSEMENT PARK

To all those who believe, are blood-washed and born-again, you have been given a ticket to enter the amusement park. You didn't have to pay for it. All you had to do was believe when the ticket was offered to you by the one who did pay for it, that you could enter the park because it had already been paid for. There were no strings attached, all you had to do was receive it and enter. This ticket admits one and entitles you to all the enjoyment you can handle while in the park. It is your right and the right of all who receive Christ, to be happy and to enjoy life in their salvation.

We all (every born-again believer) have the option to walk around or ride and see the attractions. All of the activities are included. It's simply up to you to decide which ones you will participate in or what rides you will ride while there. Your level of enjoyment and adventure while you are in the park is totally up to you. Some will get on rides and some will not. Those who ride will opt to avoid certain rides. They won't even get in line because the line is too long and they don't want to wait. Maybe there is a heat wave and the sun is beaming. Some will sweat it out, drink their fluids and keep on riding or standing in lines for rides. Others will nearly faint from the heat and cease all activity to go find a place in the shade to wait until the time of heat has passed.

Some will discipline themselves and get in that long line and wait to ride the major attraction - the roller coaster - because they want the benefit of the experience while on the ride and the joy that follows after the ride is over. Through extreme heat they will stand, through people cutting in line they will stand because they tell themselves "when I get to the front of this line and it's my turn to ride, the joy I will have afterward will have made it well worth the wait."

Some want to ride the major attractions and roller coasters because they want the same feeling as the coaster riders. But the line is too long and they don't want to wait. They allow their impatience to send them seeking quick fixes on shorter lines or less bumpy or thrilling rides. They settle for the merry-go-round (the same-old) because, well, it does offer some enjoyment and the wait is minimal. From there they will get in line for the bumper cars and from there the Ferris wheel. Understand that all of the rides are good because they are all a part of the amusement park, but all of the rides do not give the ultimate amusement park experience (in the kingdom, position seekers and church hoppers generally posses these character traits). These are the ones who will watch those come off of the roller coaster elated, excited, rejuvenated and wanting more and envy the great joy they have. They forget that while they were running from short line to short line that they scoffed the patient ones. They don't recall how they kept reiterating how dumb it was for the coaster riders to wait so long for one experience when they could've had several like them.

(That goes out to of all my sanctified singles waiting on the right one - you caught that revelation! NOW REJOICE!).

They don't want to remember that the fear of higher heights and deeper depths on the roller coaster kept them from getting in the line or caused them to move out of the line after only a short time waiting. They forget that the heights and depths of that roller coaster were equally, if not more, frightening to the coaster riders but they stayed and they waited because they wanted more out of their amusement park experience than just the merry-go-round, the bumper cars and the Ferris wheel. Are you with me?

And now they (the merry-go-rounders) have a problem with those who were patient because they envy their joy, their success and their new level of anointing. They don't want to be reminded that while the coaster riders pressed for that more-than-minimal experience, they (the merry-go-rounders) opted for an easier route.

The coaster riders fasted while the merry-go-rounders ate steak. The coaster riders prayed at 5:00 a.m. while the merry-go-rounders slept an extra three hours. The coaster riders shut in and the merry-go-rounders slept in. The coaster riders gave until it hurt and the merry-go-rounders saved for a rainy day. The coaster riders did what it took to get in the face of God, touch His heart and move Him into their world by creating a constant atmosphere of praise for Him to dwell in.

The coaster riders exchanged talking for Tehillah, they exchanged fussing and screaming for Shabaching, they broke through their hell with Hallelujah, and they traded in crying and complaining for thanking and praising!

You who would dare to take that extra step - you're seeing the attractions. You're riding the rides, and when promotion time comes, you get in line for the roller coaster and you wait to ride it. You maximize your time and instead of taking a walk in the park you are running through it with child-like enthusiasm and great joy!

Don't let fear, frustration or impatience keep you from getting the full enjoyment of your time in the park (life).

YOU ARE NOT ALONE.

As believers we are all in the amusement park together. There are others taking the ride with you and having similar experiences. There are the operators or those who have been put in position to keep an eye on the mechanisms of the roller coaster to make sure it operates safely while you are on board. So why be in the park and see the joy and adventure available to you but never experience it because of fear or impatience?

Why not take God up on his offer for you to receive promotion and get more out of life? No one is going to force you to ride anything. It's up to you. You can strap in and go for the ride of a lifetime or you can just walk around and watch others reap the full benefits of their time in the amusement park.

Yes, roller coasters have lots of sudden movements, speed changes, highs, lows, twists, turns, bumps, ups and downs, but a roller coaster without the extremities and dynamics is simply a ride on a choo-choo train. And in the end all would say that the ride could not have been what it was without them.

The story of your adventure in the park will be based on what you choose to do while you are there.

Chapter Twenty-Three
CHANGE THE WAY YOU THINK

"CHANGE YOUR MIND AND YOU CHANGE YOUR LIFE" - KELLY PRICE.

I don't know if anybody said it before me, but since I did say it and have for some time now, I'm calling it mine. This became my personal motto for life a few years back. I needed to make changes in my life with weight and health. I needed to make changes at home and in my personal life and I also needed to make changes in my relationship with Jesus Christ. The more I applied it, the more it took root in my spirit and the greater results I saw all around. I began to prioritize things differently. Things that once seemed so important couldn't even get an audience with my brain. As it helped me, I wanted to share it. So I made it a habit of telling fans at the end of my concerts and at the end of every show, when I traveled with plays and other tours. I even said in TV and print interviews that no matter what you are trying to do in your life, if you change your mind you will change your life! The mind is that powerful. Once you begin to believe that you can do a thing you will do it!

Changing the way you think. This is not easy - especially if you have the tendency to be pessimistic. Although many of us would deny being pessimistic, more of us are than will admit it or possibly even know it. For so long we have been programmed to believe that good things won't happen to us. Or how about the ones that are afraid for too many good things to happen because they feel like something bad has to follow it?

They convince themselves that it has to be that way in order to maintain some type of cosmic balance in the universe or something. You feel like "prosperity isn't for me" or "I have to just take the hand life dealt me and play it." Now, I know a little something about cards and I know that when the hand looks a little ugly or if too many kinds of the same card keep showing up, you shuffle the deck really well! The same must be done in our thinking about life and the way we speak. The mind is very powerful and can be dangerous to the believer in their walk if they have not learned how to bring it under the subjection of the Holy Spirit. If you can change the way you think the rest comes easy.

THE JOURNEY OF YOUR THOUGHTS

Thoughts travel a road before we can ever see the effects of them. First, they find a point of entry - usually the eye gate or the ear gate. From there, the thought goes into your head and you begin to think about it, you dwell on it. If these thoughts are negative and are not rebuked and expelled from the mind, they begin to settle into your heart. Once settled in your heart the thoughts take a detour and begin to come out of the mouth, evidencing what's going on inside.

For out of the abundance of the heart the mouth speaketh
MATT 12:34B.

When something has filled your heart, you don't just say it once but you tend to say it over and over and over again. From the repetitions of the mouth, whatever is being said makes its way into your spirit. Whatever can connect with your spirit will become a part of your personality. From the spirit it then moves in to the realm of your secret place within your soul and as it grows it moves from being a personality flaw to a character flaw. It becomes a part of your character. We cannot stop thoughts from coming into our heads, but we have been given a course of action in the Word that we can take to pluck these things out of our minds before they have time to pack luggage and start their journey to our souls.

This is a quick "to-do" list that you can run by yourself everyday and practice to make sure you are on the right path to changing the way you think. Right now speak a word to yourself and say, "I will begin to break the cycle of stinkin' thinkin' today!"

1.) Rebuke negative thoughts immediately.
Do not play with this. You cannot control bad things from popping into your head. But when they do, do not allow any time to pass for you to dwell on the thought or even to consider it. At the moment you have a negative thought you must, without delay, begin to rebuke it and plead the blood of Jesus over your mind. Tell the devil he will not make your mind a home for his filth and negativity.

2.) Think good thoughts.
Not *if* you don't feel like it but *especially if* you don't feel like it. Counter the bad thoughts by flooding your mind with good thoughts. Force it if you have to.

Finally, brethren, whatsoever things are true, whatsoever things are honest, whatsoever things are just, whatsoever things are pure, whatsoever things are lovely, whatsoever things are of good report; if there be any virtue and if there be any praise, think on these things.
PHILIPPIANS 4:8

That is a part of the concept of being a cold-blooded praiser. For example, rather than thinking about how aggravating it is to have to take the bus to work because you don't have a car, think about the fact that instead of sitting behind the wheel on the highway in traffic being aggravated, you have extra time to rest or read your Word and commune with God before arriving to work. The more you force this way of thinking the more it will become a part of you and it will get easier and easier until it becomes second nature and you automatically begin to do it.

3.) Speak only good things.
Speak good things only while in this mood and mood shift. Take the good thoughts from your head and begin to speak them from your mouth. This may come out as a praise or song or exhortation but it needs to come out of your mouth in some way so that it can take shape in the atmosphere. It is not easy to do, especially if you haven't been doing it, but whatever you practice you will eventually perfect.

Speaking to yourself in psalms and hymns and spiritual songs, singing and making melody in your heart to the Lord; Giving thanks always for all things unto God and the Father in the name of our Lord Jesus Christ
EPHESIANS 5:19-20

Using this same example, after thinking about being able to relax and ride rather than drive - a mood change should begin to ensue. If it doesn't, that's fine too because sometimes it takes things to be heard aloud to have impact. Begin to tell yourself God is good because in the middle of financially difficult times when many need jobs and don't have them, God has blessed me to have a job and the health and strength to go and work this job everyday. God is good to me.

4.) Thank God
Tell God "thank you" for helping you change what could've ended up as another bad seed planted in your spiritual garden and adding to the already thick patches of complaint weeds that need to be burned and destroyed.

5.) Repeat as needed.
This is like taking medication. The only difference is if you overdose on this it won't kill you but it will add to every aspect of your life.

Now, there is nothing else that you need to do. The words and the thoughts will do the rest. Keep filling your head with good things. Keep finding good things to say aloud so that your spirit will catch hold of it. The thoughts and the words will make their journey through you and you'll see the difference in not just your personality, but also in your character.

There is one last point that is of critical importance and must be made concerning this. You must understand this next thing to understand the difference between a God thought and a thought born of other influences. For every true thing that God has for you, there is a false or a counterfeit thing that will be presented by the enemy. Sometimes thoughts that come to you will seem right and true, but they are not. One sure way to know the difference is that when God presents something to you, He will present it to your mind and your spirit will bear witness clearing the way for your mind to think it through to completion. From that point on, your thoughts will make their way on the journey through you to become attached to your innermost parts.

The devil however, cannot present things to you that will bear witness in your spirit. He cannot enter your spirit because you are a spirit-filled child of God. He is not authorized to do so. He has to find another point of entry through the flesh such as the eye gate or the ear gate as I mentioned before. These gates lead to your mind and many times go unchallenged because we, the sanctified children of the Most High, have a tendency to like peeking or listening when we think no one knows. This is how we get into trouble. Any thought that pops in your head did not just pop up there. It came as the result of something you saw or heard even if it was a long time ago.

So God speaks to your mind with the witness of the spirit and the devil speaks to your mind with the assistance of the gates (eyes and ears). Your spirit cannot become corrupted unless what the devil presents to your mind goes unchallenged and is allowed to travel the path to your secret place.

The counterfeits sure look real sometimes. But the fake will always have some type of malfunction. For this reason I advise you to watch as well as pray!

Chapter Twenty-Four
SURVIVOR OR OVERCOMER?

This chapter snuck its way into my book. I found myself hearing and seeing and reading so much about the topic of surviving difficulties that I wanted to take a stab at it myself. Now when I hear the word *survive,* my mind automatically goes to coming out alive. However, we as Christians have to know that there is more to coming through trials and tribulations than just barely making it out alive, so I decided there has to be more to this and I began digging.

I have heard a lot of people talking about surviving lately. People are giving seminars, teaching classes and even preaching sermons and I love it all! Both in and out of the church you have those who are teaching and imparting wisdom on how to make it through the rough times in life.

Gloria Gaynor recorded a song many years ago that is now a classic, called "I Will Survive". Destiny's Child recorded a song more recently which can be hailed a new classic called "Survivor". In each of these songs the writers penned instances in which circumstances came against them that should've made them throw in the towel and give up on life, love and their dreams, but they held on and survived their obstacles. I have come through many things in life that if it were not for the extra stuff that God put in me I would have gone crazy or even decided that life wasn't worth living a long time ago. That coupled with the fact that so many people are talking about being a survivor, intrigued me to embark on my own research of the topic.

As defined in Webster's New World Dictionary and Thesaurus the word *survivor* is a noun that means *one that survives or someone that is regarded as capable of surviving changing conditions, misfortune.* Further study of the root word *survive* gives you the definition *to remain alive or in existence after.*

Interesting.

The word *overcomer* is also a noun and as defined in Webster's, means *one that overcomes.* Further study of the root word *overcome* gives this definition: *to get the better of in competition.* To MASTER, PREVAIL OVER OR SURMOUNT. TO WIN!

Very interesting.

In both instances, I have taken the root and defined it. In doing so, the only thing necessary to understand the definition of each word is to take the definition of the root and apply it as if it were the characteristic or personality trait of an individual. Then, you have your definition of each word.

Survivors are amazing individuals who should be celebrated and applauded for their courage. Survivors are individuals who have many times had to perform courageous acts while facing great adversity or even life threatening situations. Just think about it - when you hear the word *survivor,* it is often connected to some great tragic happening that describes exactly what it was that the individual survived.

rape survivor
cancer survivor
abuse survivor
incest survivor
sole survivor

Each of these is connected to horrible things that destroy lives. It is an amazing thing that anyone could and does walk away from any of these situations. However, there was something that I was looking for in my research of survivors that I could not find anywhere and was very troubling to me. That was evidence of victory or redemption in connection with being a survivor. It was nowhere to be found. So I went to my Strong's Concordance for a little help in trying to locate the word *survivor* or *survive* in the Bible, but I couldn't find it there either. Not in past present or future tense can this word be found. So, now the questions that arise in my mind are, who said I'm a survivor? Who said I should call myself a survivor? Should I even associate with that? Should I want to?

This was starting to become more intriguing, so I continued.

The first thing I took note of is that the word *overcomer* doesn't have any medical terminologies or socially recognizable nicknames with which to be commonly associated like the word *survivor* does. The very next thing I notice in my comparison of the two words is that although both words speak of making it through a period of difficulty, *overcome* is the only one of the two that speaks of coming through the difficult time with a victorious outcome. Whereas *survive/survivor* does not. Further investigation of the word *overcomer/overcome* reveals to me that this word IS in the Bible in several tenses of the English language.

The Lord says of the born again believer: *And they (us, the saints, and the children of God) OVERCAME him (Satan) by the blood of the lamb and by the word of their testimony.*
REVELATIONS 12:11

The Lord says of Himself: *These things I have spoken unto you that in me ye might have peace. In the world ye shall have tribulation: but be of good cheer; I have over come the world.*
JOHN 17:33

The Lord says of Himself and we who are born again: *To him that overcometh will I grant to sit with me in my throne, even as I also overcame, and am set down with my Father in His throne.*

REVELATIONS 3:21

The Word says of us: *For whatsoever is born of God overcometh the world: and this is the victory that overcometh the world, even our faith. Who is he that overcometh the world, but he that believeth that Jesus is the son of God.*
I JOHN 5:4-5

It is evident that survivors possess the natural ability to come through tough times alive. It is also evident that overcomers possess supernatural ability to survive with victory. What is the difference? There are many who have survived acts of violence towards them and lived to tell about it, but are still tortured by the memory and the scars - whether they be emotional ones that cannot be seen or physical ones that are visible. Survivors tell their stories while memorializing and celebrating their battle scars as medals of honor and proof that they have been through a war of some kind.

Overcomers give testimonies of the mortal dangers they have faced and how the God of their salvation was faithful and brought them through. They celebrate because although they were beaten and bruised, they have no emotional scars to show because as an overcomer, they have been completely healed from the wounds that were associated with their tribulation. There is no torture associated with memories because the Father's gift to His children is the peace that He promises to give each and everyone of us. It's His peace, perfect peace, the peace that surpasses any of man's understanding.

It's simply this: because I live and have a will, I can survive. Because I live and am a child of God and have given my will over to His will, I am an overcomer.

EXCLUSIVITY
I have drawn the conclusion that it is the born-again believer and no one else who has the exclusive right to take on the name of *overcomer* and apply it to their own name. This is clearly a prerequisite to attach this name to

your own as outlined in the scripture references. God meant for us to be more than survivors. He knew that there would be many adverse things that we would face in life. It is not His will to have any of us even associate as merely survivors. There is no victory in it and He, the Lord has promised us and given us the victory over and over again. The Lord does not deliver us from situations to leave us with wounds and scars that need to be licked, but He heals us and takes the sting out of the memory so that rather than telling stories of survival, we are giving our testimonies of overcoming! I understand that it is a popular phrase and it sounds good but I remind you of the things I have shown you about words and their power. There are too many Christians walking around with the mentality of a survivor - to make it through. It's time that we as the children of God adjust our thinking and begin to see ourselves for who we truly are. We need to confess that we are not survivors but overcomers, which is what our God intends for us to be. This is why the Word tells us that we are more than conquerors through Him (Jesus Christ) that loved us.

Many may not agree with me on this next one but I am going to say it anyway. I believe that to merely see yourself as a survivor is to accept the devil's counterfeit for your life. The attitude of the survivor is "if I can just make it through". The attitude of the overcomer is "I'm coming out of this thing with victory!" DON'T ACCEPT ANYTHING LESS THAN WHAT GOD HAS PROMISED YOU AS HIS CHILD! He never said anything in His Word to you about surviving the world or surviving tribulation. He did say overcome. God wants you to not only come through or survive great trials but He wants you to master and surmount, prevail over and win every one of your battles.

I have learned that I don't want anything that God does not want for me. God doesn't want me to survive - He's ordained for me to overcome the world. That means everything in the world!
Change the way you see yourself coming through trials. The Hebrew boys did not survive the furnace, they overcame it. Because when they came out there was no evidence in them that pointed to the fact that they'd ever

been in the fire.

I believe that all of the names associated with *survivor* that I mentioned before need to be changed. Especially if you - as a believer - have the testimony of those experiences and having received deliverance and the healing virtue of Jesus Christ in your life for that situation. Speak victory to yourself as an overcomer and change the name you wear. When you testify or talk to someone about your circumstance, change your language. Speak it to yourself first so it will register in your spirit. Too often we take on the identity that's been given to us through society or family and friends. Now is the time to stand up and speak out and go by the name your Father gave you.

You are not a Cancer Survivor you are a CANCER OVERCOMER!

You are not an Incest Survivor you are an INCEST OVERCOMER!

You are not a Rape Survivor you are a RAPE OVERCOMER!

You are not an Abuse Survivor you are an ABUSE OVERCOMER!

It is important that you understand that I have nothing against those who call themselves survivors and speak proudly of it. I honestly believe that there is an ability to survive that God Himself put in each of us. But I also believe that surviving is just a stepping stone to the greater portion of victory that God has for His children. I believe that greater portion is called overcoming.

I also believe what the Word of God says that for those of us who will lean not to our own understanding (especially in times of tribulation) but in all our ways acknowledge Him (for what we must do to make it through and survive) that He will direct our path (from survival to overcoming). This is your exclusive right as a blood-washed born-again child of God!

The more you speak it, the more it will register in your spirit.

Remember this: Survivors are instinctive. Overcomers are distinctive.

You are God's child of distinction. You are more than a survivor. You are an overcomer.

Chapter Twenty-Five
ALL OR NOTHING

Many of you - before you ever picked up this book - had already been feeling a pull from within to make changes in your life. Maybe you don't really know what it is, but you know it's there. For many of you, it's the reason you even bothered to read this book. For some of you, that feeling has come as a result of reading this book. It's the little uneasy feeling you get in your belly or the antsy thing that overtakes you when you have too much time alone with your thoughts. Sleep now escapes many of you and insomnia has become your all-night hang out partner. Maybe you are doing things or living a certain way and you know that it's wrong or questionable, at best. Maybe you are not blatantly doing things that are wrong but you still know that something is missing. You know there is a void somewhere in your life and you just can't seem to get it filled. I have wonderful news for you. You are not going crazy or experiencing a breakdown of any kind. What you are feeling is called conviction and it is a good thing. In fact it's a wonderful thing. It is God speaking to you through your senses to make you see and feel that He's calling you and that you are missing Him and you need Him. It is a call that has gone out from Heaven and made contact with your spirit and the only way to calm yourself is for your spirit to respond to its Creator. It needs to respond to find peace.

He's calling you to return to your first love. And He is your first love. He loved you before anyone else did. He's loved you consistently and unconditionally. He's loved you enough that when you just didn't want Him - as much as it hurt - He let you go and do your own thing. But He never gave up on you. He was always nearby watching over you while hoping and waiting for the day that you would think about Him and want Him in your life. The thing is that He wants all of you. He's always felt that way, *all or nothing*. He doesn't want to have to share you with immorality, negativity or bad habits. And so after months and years of watching you and seeing the road you've taken and knowing that you are yearning for more and searching for completion, He has chosen now as the appointed time that you should come together. So He's calling you. Not forceful. Not pushy. Just a call. Can you feel the slight discomfort?

The fact that you are experiencing such unrest in your soul lets you know that you have been on God's mind. You have moved from His mind and are now in the mouth of God. He's calling your name and your inner being is reacting, which is causing your body to make you feel uneasy. This means that you are very precious to Him so He took the time to stop and let you know that He wants to talk to you. And you can do it right now where you are.

If you know that you have fallen out of communication with your Heavenly Father you can reconnect with Him right now. No matter what you've done, it's not too late for you. In fact, right now is perfect. The Bible says the day you hear His voice, harden not your heart. He's talking to you now.

Talk back to Him - read this aloud.

Lord Jesus. I am a sinner and I come to You now asking You for forgiveness. I am sorry for all the wrong things I've done in my life. Forgive me for the things that I am aware of and the things that I am unaware of. I acknowledge that Jesus Christ is the Son of God and I believe that He died for my sins and rose again so I can live a happy, blessed, sin-free and guilt-free life. I know that I can only live that life in You, Jesus. Wash me from the inside out. I yield my will to Your will. Any habits that I might have that would not be pleasing to You I place them in Your hands and ask You now for the strength I need to stop and never return to them. I thank You for loving me enough to allow me to feel conviction in my heart to turn to You. Lord, I have now confessed with my mouth and I believe in my heart that You have forgiven me and I am saved. Thank You for saving me! Thank You for saving me! Thank You for saving me! AMEN.

AND IT'S JUST THAT SIMPLE!!! NO RITUALISTIC PRACTICES IN ORDER TO BE BORN AGAIN. JUST THE PRAYER OF FAITH. IF YOU SAID IT AND BELIEVED WHAT YOU SAID, YOU ARE NOW SAVED!

I am so happy and proud that you would make the decision to receive Jesus as your Lord and Savior. Your life will never be the same from this time forth. Condemnation has removed itself from you in that quick of an instance. SEE ROMANS 8:1.

Now, what I want you to do as you continue to thank God for saving you is to let go of all the guilt and shame you have been carrying around. You are not that same person anymore so you shouldn't be carrying the baggage of that person.

Thank the Lord and let it go.

Thank Jesus and forgive yourself as your Heavenly Father has forgiven you.

Thank Him and keep thanking Him.

The work is already done. It was done when Jesus Christ went to Calvary.

The Lord promises that He would take your sins and throw them in the sea of forgetfulness never to remember them again. God doesn't remember them and is no longer holding that to your charge. Now He wants you to forget about the past and reach toward your new future in Him. SEE PHILIPPIANS 3:13-14 - it's a good one, I promise!

Chapter Twenty-Six
THE MICROWAVE MENTALITY

This chapter and the one that follows this can and should be read by all, but it is specifically written for those who are new Christians with the hopes of offering you insight to this new time in your life. This chapter will - in plain English using everyday comparisons - help you understand the importance of being processed and raised in the faith. Being new in Christ is an exciting time. There is a zeal that always accompanies being newly converted, however it is important that you understand that because you are new, you are spiritually like a baby and you must be nourished and fed so you can grow and be strong. For this to occur you must be diligent and persistent in your walk, your mind must be totally made up to not go back to things that are bad or possibly compromising to your new faith. You MUST BE connected to a BIBLE-BASED church and strong people who will help you when you get discouraged or when it seems like you want to go back in the other direction (back to your old life).

You must have patience while being processed and cultivated to help you avoid certain pitfalls. Many of those who have gone before you were either improperly nourished or grew impatient with the process and moved too quickly into areas of spirituality or ministry that they were not ready to tackle. Please do not fall victim to this very familiar and often successful trap that the enemy has set up for babes in Christ. Satan is cunning and he will try to use your eagerness to grow and progress against you if you are not careful.

It is imperative that you read and really understand everything that it spoken to you in this portion of the book. The type of Christian I am about to explain is dangerous to themselves and also dangerous to others. You may have even encountered Christians like this in the past and, as a result, been misinformed about things that are crucial to your faith walk. The goal here is to stop the madness so we can have healthy and mature Christians who can help grow and mature other healthy and mature Christians.

The world today is extremely fast paced. Everything needs to happen yesterday. There is high-speed internet, fast money, fast cars, and fast food. We want what we want when we want it and anything less is unacceptable. We learn as we reach for success to resort to the popular cliché's: "The early bird gets the worm," "You snooze, you lose," "You slow, you blow." It is the way of the world today and it is what I like to refer to as the *microwave mentality*. Getting things more quickly and efficiently is not a bad thing, it's quite convenient but I think we can all agree that ALL things need not be rushed.

Things like:
- time spent with loved ones
- choosing a mate
- eating a good meal
- cooking a meal
- any life-altering or important decision

THE MICROWAVE EXPERIENCE

I am fairly certain that everyone reading this book has knowledge of the microwave oven or at least knows of its existence. Just in case … the microwave oven is that rectangular object in many kitchens that can be used to cook or reheat food very rapidly. Microwave ovens are electrically powered and function by something called microwave heating.

I must - before laying out this spiritual parallel - give the full scientific definition of certain terms so you can receive the maximum benefit of this comparison.

Microwave as defined by Webster's New World Dictionary of Science is *an electromagnetic wave with a wavelength in the range 0.3 to 30 cm/0.1 inch to 12 inches, or 300-300,000 megahertz (between radio waves and infrared radiation). Microwaves are used in radar, radio broadcasting and in microwave heating and cooking.*

Microwave heating as defined by the same reference tool, is *heating by means of microwaves. Microwave ovens use this form of heating for the RAPID COOKING or REHEATING of foods, where heat is generated throughout the food simultaneously. If the food is not heated completely there is a danger of bacterial growth that may lead to FOOD POISONING. Industrially microwave heating is used for destroying insects in grain and enzymes in processed food, pasteurizing and sterilizing liquids, and drying timber and paper.*

It is my opinion - and I will say the opinion of most - that food is best either hot or cold. When it's hot, it is robust and is saturated in full-bodied flavor. When it is cold, there is still flavor, although the flavor seems to be trapped and suspended or frozen in place rather than running through the food. It's cold, but it's consistent. However, lukewarm food tends to be very uneven in texture, consistency, temperature and flavor - a little flavor over here, a little bland over there, cold over here, hot over there, firm over here and soft over there. All in all, a very unpleasant eating experience.

The microwave oven is well known for producing this kind of unpleasant result with food. The same is true for the babe in Christ. When you avoid the process of being seasoned and slow cooked to perfection in your spirituality, something phenomenal but very wrong happens with the finished product. You come out a lot faster than the babe who goes through the oven but you take on the spiritual attributes of what can be likened to a frozen dinner prepared in the microwave. You are hot and on fire when you come out and you look good and even smell pleasing, however because your process was not slow and thorough but produced by fast moving particles going through your spirit (microwaves) fueled by impatience - you don't have lasting qualities. You, like the microwave meal, have a very short time in which you will be of edible quality. Whatever nourishment that can come from you has to come quickly before you rubberize or harden. Then there is the very real danger that you, like the microwave meal, could become poisonous to those who receive of your substance because you were not heated completely. Going through the spiritual microwave will always leave the new Christian uneven and eventually hard.

If you want results like grandma got, you must do the things grandma did - which means the microwave is not the way to go. Think of the results grandma (and those after her who have received her wisdom) would get when cooking that pot roast the old way. Now compare them to the results that would come if that same piece of meat was placed in a bowl and stuck inside the microwave. Not too appetizing huh?

Let's see why:

There are several problems that arise when you microwave your food.
1. If you do not leave your food in long enough, your result is a lukewarm meal with uneven consistency, temperature and flavor. The results are the same of the Christian who has the microwave experience and cuts the heating cycle short in an effort to get in and out quickly. They are lukewarm.

   To learn what God feels about lukewarm Christians see Revelations 3:14-22.

2. If you do leave the food in long enough to remove the cold spots and avoid being lukewarm, your result is still an unevenly cooked meal with hot spots in some places and scalding hot spots in others that will burn you.

The same is true spiritually. You may avoid coming out lukewarm, however, you are still a danger to the Body of Christ. You are uneven and have hotspots in hidden places. These hotspots are areas in which you are misinformed because you have not been trained properly. This is the training you would have received while being slowly processed. You are already burned, and as you move forward, will go on to burn those who receive spiritually from you.

Also, as babes in Christ, bouncing back from these kinds of burns is extremely difficult. They can cause lasting damage that only the healing of God, the guidance of your pastor and the senior seasoned saints will be able to bring you back from. MICROWAVES ARE NOT SAFE FOR BABIES OR THEIR FOOD.

3. If you leave your food in the microwave too long it comes out inedible by completely hardening before you ever get to eat it.

    Spiritually this is the one who completely overdoes the microwave experience. They'll spend a little extra time in the microwave thinking, "I get a little extra so maybe I'll last longer than the others, but it still doesn't take as long as the oven so I still can move on a little faster." This person is often so hard that they are impermeable and cannot be penetrated by anything or anyone because they feel they know it all. They cannot be taught. The only hope for this individual is to be broken and to have to go back to the altar and start again so God can soften them and make them ready to receive truth.

4. Whatever the amount of time you leave your food in the microwave, there is one certainty. If you do not eat the food quickly, it will become rubbery and inedible. This is the end result for every instance in the microwave experience. You will become rubbery and there is a good chance that you will harden. No matter what your texture is, you will not be a provider of healthy spiritual food for those you come in

contact with, which makes you a walking disaster for yourself and for others.

There is no quick turn-out. You must be patient. You must be processed. The Bible says *let patience have her perfect work.* (JAMES 1:4) You cannot reach perfection in Christ being impatient and always looking for the fast and easy way to the finish.

There is another way. It is the right way and it involves having patience and allowing the time for you to be properly developed so that you grow into the healthy and mature Christian that God wants you to be.

Chapter Twenty-Seven
SLOW COOKED SANCTIFICATION

THE PERSONAL TOUCH
When it comes to making meals, anyone who knows me knows that I love to cook and I love to feed people. I get high from watching people eat my food and stuff themselves until they cannot move! My understanding is that this love of the culinary arts was passed on to me from my dad who was a chef by trade. Believe it or not, as much of a modern-day girl as I am, many of my ways are very old-fashioned. For instance - the methods of cooking that I use are the things I learned from watching my grandmother. As a result, slow and easy is my cooking method of choice. I prefer using my hands to give the personal touch. To me it feels better and it tastes better. Can you believe that I still cut and chop vegetables and herbs by hand? I own a couple of food processors and electric choppers but my attitude is simply by the time I get it set up and prepped I can have it all chopped myself. AND I LOVE TO DO IT! Convection ovens and microwaves are wonderful. They knock minutes - sometimes hours - off of cooking times. I look back now and I ask myself, "How did we live without them?" WE WERE CAVEMEN! But I still prefer the slower process of a roaster pan cooking in the oven where, by the strength of the aroma, you can tell the exact stage of preparation your dish is in. And when your dish is finished you know that it is done and it is cooked thoroughly with equal consistency and full flavor throughout. There are no hot or cold spots to speak of and no rawness when food is prepared in an oven because every part of the dish is receiving equal amounts of heat.

THE PROCESS

This old school method of cooking is a great parallel to the way the old saints nurtured and cared for new Christians. They watched out for them and protected them. They prayed with them and for them. They taught them how to pray for themselves and others. They taught them and trained them. They seasoned them with the Word of God and broke down the parts that were too tough or indigestible for them. They helped them understand the Bible and how it applied to their lives. They reinforced things over and over again, even when the baby saint felt they knew the ins and outs of certain things. They made sure that they were strong before allowing them to take off and try to save the world. They held the growing Christian back at times, even when the baby saint felt they were ready to spread their wings. The older saints knew that they were merely adolescents and, although they had the appearance of a grown-up Christian, their minds were wrestling between babe and adult (sounds like the teen years). This is the danger zone. This is when you, the newly-converted Christian, may want to say, "I got this! I've been here six months now. I've been faithful and I've done everything I've been asked to do. I've been coming to prayer, coming to church services and coming to Bible study. I know the answers to most of the questions in Bible study and Sunday school. When is someone going to trust me to teach a class, when is someone going to trust me to head a program or be an inspirational speaker at one of the services? I believe God has called me to the ministry. I want to get up in the pulpit and talk to the church. I have a testimony worth telling and it needs to be heard. When do I get my turn?"

This is the time when you who must tell yourself, "I don't know it all and I must trust those who are watching over my soul." This is the time that you must recognize that flying too soon could result in a nasty fall and cause lasting damage, or worse - lead you back into sin. This is the time when you must pray even more and ask God to keep you. This is the trap of the Microwave Mentality! You must be willing to be slow processed. You must tell yourself to take your time and learn. This point in your walk is not about holding you back. Think of the Olympians who race. Those runners understand that in a race, once they take off running, that's it! They are gone. The key to being able to run until the end for them is having received the proper conditioning (mind and body) before the race starts so they don't get cramps and fall or get tired and be forced off to the side! This is the preparation of champions!

That is the preparation you need for a lifetime faith walk. The old saints called it "growing in grace" and they did whatever was necessary to help you grow in grace. Now I realize I make a lot of references to the senior saints in church and this is because that is what I was exposed to primarily when I was being raised. Those are my memories and experiences. I do realize, however, that a lot of young people and new Christians are not as comfortable with being so free with older people in general because of generational differences in thinking. I understand that completely and I often felt that way myself while growing up. It is important that you, the babe in Christ, understand that in the Christian walk, being up in age is not the only qualification for being labeled a senior or seasoned Christian. It is strictly related to the amount of time you have been saved combined with the experiences and overcoming victories you've had during your faith walk. That means for you, a 25- or 30-year-old person could be considered seasoned and would make a great prayer partner and mentor for you as you start your journey. Your pastor or one of your church leaders are always best with helping you find someone who can be that mentor for you.

We are our brothers' keepers and that understanding rests deep within the heart and mind of those who are in Christ. We accept the responsibility to watch out for each other in matters of life and in the faith. We want to see wholeness for each other in every aspect of life. (SEE I THESSALONIANS 5:11-23)

These are the living examples of Christians you want around you to mentor you into healthy living - mind, body and spirit. They will help you become what you need to be. They'll help you develop temperance and all the other fruits of the spirit, which is the slow-roasted, oven-cooked mentality of grandma. (SEE GALATIANS 5:22-23)

RESULTS OF THE PROCESS (OVEN)

I know it will be tempting at times to try your hand at things you will see others around you doing. You may even see those who are still considered babes in Christ or in the adolescent stages of their Christianity doing things that you want to do. It may even look like they are doing well. But please don't be fooled. You must go through the process. Refusal to receive instruction and go all the way through the process is directly linked to having a spirit of pride. The Bible tells us that *pride goes before destruction and a haughty spirit before a fall.* (PROVERBS 16:18)

Sometimes it will seem frustrating, especially if those around you seem to be sprinting ahead of you. Just stay prayerful and keep your ears open to hear what God will say to you about you. You'll understand that you don't need to rush to come out of the process (oven) because you take the risk of being undercooked, thereby becoming poisonous - possibly even deadly - to anyone that you would try to feed the Word of God to. So you stay in the oven and get slow-cooked to perfection and when you came out you'll be well seasoned and full of flavor and hot like fire for Jesus. You'll smell wonderful and look good and everywhere you go, people will want to taste of what ever it is that made you so robust!

The slow-cooked Christian is hot and on fire. They are excited about God's goodness and they want everyone to know it. They have been well nourished and because they have been well nourished they can move on in ministry and deeper areas of spirituality. They have enough to share with someone else - to feed and nourish them thoroughly without experiencing a vitamin deficiency or famine in their own spirituality. They can offer another person substance without the fear of causing spiritual indigestion because they were slow processed. They were cooked slow and fed by the hands of one who was also well seasoned and cooked slow.

I know that for some this seems like you are being preached to and, to a degree, you are. My hope is that you (especially the new Christian) would take everything I've given you in these last two chapters and commit them to your heart so that you will be aware of these signs of frustration and know how to combat them when they show their ugly faces.

Again, I must warn you that the way the microwave mentality begins to set in is through the innocence and zeal that comes with being a newly converted Christian. This is why most people don't catch it or even think that they are wrong. They tell themselves, "I'm excited about Jesus and I want to do all I can for Him so I can't be wrong." Again, the enemy uses this very innocence and tries to turn it into something ugly. The Bible tells us that there is a way that seems right to us, but in the end, is judgment. Now that you know about one of the most common and sinister pitfalls set up for the baby Christian by Satan himself, you are armed (with your knowledge) and can now fight.

Chapter Twenty-Eight
LET'S GET NAKED!!

YES, LET'S GET NAKED!
I know you are probably saying to yourself, "This girl has gone off the deep end!'

Well come along and jump with me!

When I say get naked I'm talking about becoming so spiritually free that we can be honest and unashamed. It's time that we all learn how to be more real with ourselves, with God and with each other.

NAKEDNESS - God's Plan From the Beginning

Naked is the way we were intended to be. I know we all love our Versace, Sean John, RocaWear, Gucci, D&G, Armani, St. John, etc. I don't think you love it more than I do, but it's the truth. Naked was God's plan from the beginning. It sounds funny because we are so used to being adorned in our clothes but when Adam and Eve were in the Garden of Eden, God gave them everything they needed to live happily and abundantly and clothes were not included. They were naked! God made them and He knew they were naked, yet He did not deem it necessary for them to be covered. There was no shame felt by either of them, nor was there any indication that it was shameful by God. (See Genesis 2:25) As long as there was no sin, there was no shame in full disclosure or nakedness. The devil tricked Eve and she was able to persuade her husband to follow her lead and disobey God, which was sin. Not until this did Adam even realize that he and Eve were not wearing clothes. In their eyes there was only beauty and purity when they looked at each other and when they allowed themselves to become a party to an act of deception, what was pure and beautiful became embarrassing and shameful. It couldn't be looked upon the same way anymore. It is the equivalent to being in a new relationship with someone. All you see is stars and Heaven. Everything is beautiful he or she can do no wrong and you are walking on cloud nine! You are so infatuated, that literally they can do no wrong. He belches and you think it's manly. She burps and to you, it's cute. Each of the individuals may have bad habits but either they are not seen or they are not a concern. But let one of you commit an act of deception in the relationship. The same things that you were blind to or not concerned about before the misdeed took place, you are now very aware of. The things you thought were cute are now annoying. You are looking at the same person, with the same looks, qualities, capabilities and habits that they have always had but their act of deception has changed the way you perceive what you have been looking at all along.

CLOTHES - God's Backup Plan (God's plan B)

When the eyes of Adam and Eve came open and their perfect visual of the world and each other came to an abrupt end, they began to look at each other and what once was beautiful and pure became shameful. There was an overwhelming desire in each of them to hide themselves from each other and God. (See Genesis 3:7). So the Bible tells us that Adam and Eve became tailors that day and sewed some fig leaves together and made outfits to cover their bodies. They needed clothes. They could not face each other naked nor could they face God. The nakedness that was once viewed as pure and beautiful, had been forever changed in the eyes of man. Our innocence was taken.

We clothe our bodies everyday. For some of us there are parts of our bodies that we are really ashamed of. So we will make sure it is not exposed at all for fear of others' reactions or just because we don't like it and we are embarrassed. For some it may be their arms (like me) or their back or even their legs. Whatever the body part is, there is something that makes you want to keep it hidden from everyone for fear of rejection or humiliation. You may not even know for certain that the reaction from others will be negative, but you protect yourself by never exposing your limiting or differentiating characteristics or features. Or at least what you believe is limiting or different.

AS IT IS IN THE NATURAL, SO IT IS IN THE SPIRITUAL

I remember my mother often quoting her familiar saying to my sisters and I when we were growing up - "as it is in the natural, so it is in the spiritual," The more I live life and watch the turns it takes, I constantly make comparisons and can say with certainty that this is a true statement. Insecure people try to cover things about their bodies that they are ashamed of for fear that it will bring negative reaction or draw criticism or cause them to be alienated or unloved by others. Adam and Eve becoming ashamed of their bodies in the Garden of Eden was just the beginning of what Satan intended to be the superficial part of an issue that would plague man throughout time. The clothes issue was just the beginning. After the purity of nakedness was stripped from us naturally, the next step was to do it spiritually.

The devil has stolen our ability to be 100 percent open with each other. We are plagued with fear, intimidation and insecurity about our looks, personalities, talents and abilities. There have been false standards set up in the world to make people believe that if they don't look, act or dress a certain way that they are less than another person. There are standards that say if one person has more fame, notoriety or money than the next person, their overall value as a human is greater than that person. This is a spirit of deception and it is everywhere - even in the church! As Christians, we should be able to be totally naked in front of each other, but instead we gather together, service after service, broken and emotionally worn and cannot get the help we so desperately need. We should be able to come to the church and get help for the things that plague us spiritually and emotionally at any time. There was a time when there was nothing that was deemed too shameful to come to the church and seek help for. The only thing the saints or fellow Christians needed to know was that the person coming for help sincerely wanted to change. Now there are some very twisted perceptions that keep people from being helped and all are a tragedy.

- You have those who have allowed themselves to be deceived and believe that they must come to God and to the church already cleaned up so they won't seek help in the House of God. To you I say help is available, and if you ask, the Lord will lead you to the right one who can help you. If you are still unsure, go to your Pastor or seek the guidance of someone you know lives a good solid life based on Christian principals and he or she will know who to place you with if it is not him or herself.

- You have those who have become so pious that they forget about the mess they were in before they got saved and have now become judgmental. To you I say all have sinned and come short of God's glory. All souls are precious and must be treated as such. Don't forget where God brought you from or He will remind you.

- Then there are those who simply say, "It's not my business." That is the attitude of the carnal minded. IT IS YOUR BUSINESS, EVEN IF IT IS NOT YOUR ASSIGNMENT. God will always assign someone to aid in the restoration of a brother or sister who has fallen from grace into temptation and it may not be you, however, we are to pray for one another. Somehow people have allowed that same spirit that exists outside of the body of Christ to creep in and cause division in ways that, for many Christians, is not even considered division. It's just called minding your own business. THE DEVIL IS A LIAR! And I've got news for you, soul business is everybody's business that says they are a born-again believer. If a brother or sister is in danger of losing their soul because they have fallen into sin or temptation, it is your responsibility to pray them through. You don't need to know the details of the situation to pray for it. The details are none of your business but the repairs are your business!

The Bible commands us to confess our faults one to another and pray for one another that we may receive healing (see James 5:16).

Oh, if we could only get back to this place!

When the church was in compliance with this command it did two things. It kept the playing field level so no one person could ever feel that they were better than the next. We were reminded again that all have sinned and come short of the glory of God (Romans 3:23) and it kept us praying for one another to be delivered rather talking about each other.

PRAYING FOR ONE ANOTHER INSTEAD OF TALKING ABOUT ONE ANOTHER! WHAT A CONCEPT.

It is the will of our Father that we get back to a place where we can trust each other and get totally naked, just as He always intended us to. There is nothing that we shouldn't be able to speak of among each other, especially in an effort to seek help and restoration.

Yes, this would make us vulnerable but there is no fear of vulnerability with someone that you know would go to war on your behalf and take out anything that would attempt to hurt you. We are each other's keepers. If we walk in the spirit of true holiness we could regain our nakedness. This would be nakedness without shame or fear because there would be no practices of deception among us.

It is time that we snatch this long-held victory from Satan and get back to a place where we can trust and be trusted so that we may regain our ability to be spiritually and emotionally naked with each other.

Chapter Twenty-Nine
BE THE BEST

As I begin the last chapter of this book, I think of one of the great encouragers of my life, an older woman much like a mother to me, First Lady Virginia Buchanen of Mobile, Alabama. Her words to me are always, "Kelly you are the best God's got - now be the best!"

Similar words have been heard by many of us through the years. I can remember being told even as a child, "Whatever you do, be the best at it." This is something that attached itself to my psyche and then etched itself to my soul. From that time, it has never gone away, and for the most part, has been good for me. It put a drive in me that always made me strive for perfection.

I strongly believe that we should strive to be the best at anything and everything we do. We would come out with more favorable results if we went at every assignment in life with that attitude and zeal. It doesn't matter who you are, where you are from and what you do - just do it with all of your God-given ability and strength. If you are a bus driver, be the best bus driver. If you are a teacher, be the best teacher. If you are an athlete or janitor, be the best athlete or janitor and if you are the French fry attendant at McDonald's, be the best French fry attendant that ever fried a fry!

If you are a preacher, be the best and if you are an alto in the choir, be the best. If you are a saint, please be the best saint and get all from God that your salvation entitles you to - the fruit of the spirit plus power, health, wholeness, wealth and 360 degrees of happiness. In essence, you get prosperity of the mind, body, spirit and bank account and this is all BEFORE you get to Heaven!

On the flip side of that, I have to say to all of those who are sitting in church and living a lie - or maybe not in church and not even attempting to live a saved life – that, as a sinner, you need to be the best in the life that you have chosen or you are wasting time. Listen, if you are going to Hell go in style! In fact, party hard and do all you think you are big and bad enough to do. Why waste your time as a sinner living a spiritually unfruitful life and at least not gain all that being a sinner has to offer you? You know - like the wonderful morning-after feeling when you have had too much to drink at that blast of a party you went to the night before, or the struggle of trying to keep up with all the lies you've told. How about trying to trace all the different sex partners you've had so you can let them know you are sick and that they should be tested? All in all, you have a little fun followed by a lot of consequence and after that, for all of your hard work doing the wrong thing, you still have the grand prize of eternal damnation to look forward to! Sounds pretty bad, huh? Well remember all of these things started out with a good time. Now don't get me wrong, there are many appealing things that will come your way in the sinful life. We often refer to it as "The Good Life" but every one of those good looking things are based on lies, inconsistencies, half-truths and they are only temporary. They are meant to suck you in and keep you from experiencing the real "Good Life" offered to you through Jesus Christ. The Bible tells us that *wide is the gate and broad is the way that leads to destruction* (MATTHEW 7:13).

It's wide and broad because so many choose its path. No real leaders to speak of, just a bunch of followers. Many who had leadership qualities and could've led, but did not have the guts to stand up and lead properly. All of those that could-a, should-a, would a are a bunch of followers playing leap frog right into Hell. So it really isn't anything special to take the route of sin just because others around you are doing it. The oldest excuse in the book for wrongdoing is "everybody's doing it!" And although that is the very excuse used by so many to do wrong, that is the precise reason for you not to do wrong too. Do something different! Be a trailblazer! Show people it's cool to do right and live right. Let your life be the example of the 360 degrees of happiness I mentioned earlier.

It is ultimately your decision. I am just a cheerleader on the sidelines, encouraging you to play to win! The truth is that those who serve God do so because they want to. God gave every man (and woman) a free will. You have the right to choose whether or not you want to serve the Lord and live for Him. Now, I realize that many of you who are reading this book may be new to salvation or possibly still considering it and have not made up your mind yet. I want to clear this up for you so you don't think I am encouraging you to live a wild and reckless life when I say to be the best sinner. I do, however, stand behind it when I say, "In whatever you do - be the best."

It is no secret that I grew up in church as a P.K (preacher's/pastor's kid). Because of this, I always saw things in church from the inside out and it wasn't always pretty. One of the things that confused me the most were people who would come to church every time the doors were open, sometimes even held positions of authority, but lived lives outside of the church that were completely contrary to what they acted, spoke and believed when they attended church. It takes a lot of energy to live a double life—to be involved in all of the activities of a ministry and still keep up a regular schedule of hustling, clubbing and juggling multiple mates. I say to you that you are straddling the fence. Plainly said, you are wasting your time, and although you feel you are not hurting anyone, you are wrong! You are hurting yourself and God has a problem with that.

This is to the one who is just chilling outside of the fence as well. First of all, your body is the temple of the Lord. He gave it to you as a shell, or covering, to house the inner or unseen you (your spirit and soul) for your life's journey here on Earth. In it, you are to complete the assigned tasks, or destiny of your life. In it you are to be the best!

If you abuse your body through drugs, alcohol, overeating (yes that's a sin!), improper eating (He holds you accountable for this too!), promiscuity and sexual indiscretion, among other things, you will have difficulty doing all of the things you were put on Earth to do. If you abuse your body badly enough you will NOT complete your assignments because these things will always cause you to die before your time. Secondly, Jesus loved you enough to lay down His own life to redeem yours. When you boldly make the decision that you are grown and you can do whatever you want to do and no one can do anything about it, you are telling Jesus that you really don't care that He died for you. He took beatings, was spat on in the face, lied on, tortured and killed but you just don't have time in your busy life to care. A lot of people don't see it that way because we in the church and society as a whole have become desensitized to the harsh and gruesome reality associated with the torturing and dying of our Savior. It is almost as if it's just another story we hear a few times a year when the pastor preaches about Jesus dying or during the Easter season when everybody preaches about Jesus dying. To you I say you need to remind yourself of the true sacrifice that was made for you with some visual aid. Go sit and watch Mel Gibson's "The Passion of The Christ" and awaken your sensitivity!

Again, for those of you who find yourself in the not-so-good position of straddling the fence, I'm really pressed to get through to you that when it comes to being the best, you cannot be the best at either (sinner or saint) because you are not giving either of them your all. Unless of course you are trying to be the best hypocrite!

What it really boils down to is that serving God in the beauty of holiness is an amazing thing and I encourage anyone who is looking at giving his or her life to Christ to be real about it and go all the way with it. You'll never reap the full benefits of a relationship with Christ if you're half in and half out. You can't reap the full benefits of anything else you pursue in life that way and this is certainly no different.

MY BEST WASN'T GOOD ENOUGH

People have always asked me how I get up and sing every night. My answer to that is this - "I know it is a God-given ability and much of it is deepened by my life experiences that have no choice but to surface when I sing, but the inside of me will never be able to break loose on a song without hearing the voice of my mother intensify and say, 'Girl, you better open your mouth and sing!'" Without fail, every time I get up, those words resonate from the deepest corners of my memory bank. I had to sing each time like it was my last and still do. When I write music, I pour everything that's in me out of me. This is the only way I have known to be the best. I can remember walking through Edgemere projects in Far Rockaway, New York, telling myself at six-, seven- and eight-years- old, that "I live here but I don't belong here." It almost became a chant that I would mumble to myself while walking home from school or going to the store for my mother. This ambition and determination in me has brought forth great results, and for this I'm grateful. It has taken me into the lives, hearts and homes of millions of people around the world. But there was a cost.

The flip side of this drive for perfection is that there have been times when I have set unrealistic standards for myself. When I'd fall short of those standards, I would not deal too well with it. I didn't see not reaching a goal as failure to reach the goal, but rather as me being a failure as a person. If I was giving all I had to give and pouring everything out to get the job done, and my efforts were not successful, I believed that what was in me was not good enough. Eventually this began to take its toll on me emotionally because I needed to be good enough. I needed to be the best. And for every time I wasn't, it piled another load of rejection on top of all of the other negative things I'd believed about myself since I was a young child.

Even as a child I always knew I had talent, and I always excelled in school, so I knew that I was intelligent but I always believed that I never measured up in so many other ways. I began to experience emotional burnouts early in life (in my early teens to be specific). I reached a point that even in the areas of my life that I shouldn't have questioned, like my gifts, I began to question and even resent. I went through a period of time where I wanted to hide my gift of music because I felt that it was the only reason why anyone would ever take a second look at me or want to be around me. I felt that as long as I was singing and making people feel good around me that they would always be around. I was the court jester. I wanted to stop singing but I couldn't stop singing because if I did I would be alone. I had to be the best because if I wasn't the best then the "love" that I was getting from those around me would go away.

THE BALANCING ACT

I had drive and determination and the will to survive but there was no one to say, "Kelly, you don't have to be perfect!" There was no one to tell me that it was okay to fail because there were lessons in certain failures that would carry me to heights of greatness that otherwise could never be reached. What was happening to me was that the survival instinct and overcoming tools God gave me for life were being used against me by the enemy of my soul. The Lord stepped in at a crucial point in my life to teach me that in Him there is no failure, which simply meant that all I had to do whenever I embarked upon a new task, was to do everything as unto the Lord and I always win. I'm always good enough and I'm always the best. Without that affirmation from the Lord, I could've been destroyed emotionally by the perceptions of my mind.

There is an old saying that too much of anything is no good. This is in direct conflict with the equally familiar but more popular saying that you can never have too much of a good thing. So which is it? Let's weigh it out.

Good times, celebration times, don't-worry-be-happy-times - we love them! We want life to be this way always without ever having to be concerned about adversity in any area. Enter problems (or challenges as I prefer to call them). We don't like them but every now and then they are necessary. There is a song I remember called *Through It All* that says it best. The words say *if I never had a problem I wouldn't know that God could solve them and I'd never know what faith in God could do.* God never intended that every day would be filled with sunshine. In fact He told us in the Word (Mark 10:29-30) that although He intends to bless us greatly in this lifetime just for following Him, but that those blessings would come with persecution. Balance is good for us and our Heavenly Father knows this. The blessings are coming from Him so He could very easily remove the headaches that would be imposed on us by envy-filled onlookers. But they are actually good for you. They keep you in God's face even after you have prospered and as long as you remain in God's face, you cannot help but be balanced. This principle applies to every area of life as God created it. Even in nature if you get too much sunshine and not enough rain, vegetation and plant life begin to dry up and die, drought comes and eventually animals begin to die too. If there still is no rain, people will eventually die. Rain, although accompanied by clouds which bring darkness, has its purpose in the earth and is necessary to give balance to the wonderful effects of the sunshine we love so much.

The necessity of balance is especially important in matters of spirituality. There are some Christians who convince themselves that they have become so deep that no one can reach them because they feel that no one else is on their level of spiritual deepness. What do I say about that? I gladly borrow a saying that I remember my mother using quite often – "it makes no sense to be so Heavenly minded that you are no Earthly good!" We are living here in the world and we must know how to function and communicate with people in order to live successfully, or we negate our purpose and void the testimony we'd have to reach others. If people cannot relate to us as real "down to Earth" people we make ourselves non-effective, and if you cannot reach souls, then what are you here for?

HOW CAN YOU BE THE BEST?

It is not impossible to achieve the status of being the best. It is not anything you can learn by receiving lessons or even imitating someone you consider to be the best at something. Rather, it is a calling, and if you want to be the best you must walk in that calling to the best of your natural ability and where your ability ends, God's supernatural ability takes over, gives the increase and makes up the difference all at the same time.

It took me a long time to really understand the true meaning of being the best and I want to share a few points with you that will help you understand how to walk in the calling of *the best* for your own life.

- Your beginning (family history, ethnicity, financial status, gender, or other discriminating or negative factor) does not have to determine what your end will be.
- Whatever you are trying to accomplish make sure it is in the plan of the Lord for your life and if it is, then do it as unto the Lord. IF He said it, He must sanction it and bring it to pass!
- Being the best is a calling to walk in all your days not a title to be won and worn until the next best comes along.
- Being the best is not about your ability, it is about your usability in Christ.
- Being the best is not always achieving success as man would know it but will many times look like a failure in the eyes of people.
- YOU CAN DO ALL THINGS THROUGH CHRIST WHO GIVES YOU STRENGTH!

If you can remember these few things whenever you embark on a new assignment, success is guaranteed and inevitable.

The key to what I had to learn, what you must learn, and what my wonderful mentor wanted me to know is that God already spoke it out of His mouth that I am His best. The only thing that could change that would be me - whether it is in thoughts, words or deeds. Even through severe struggle, her mission was to remind me that God had not changed His mind about what and who He made me to be. He said, "I made you the best - now be the best. Choose to overcome, choose life and not death, choose to win and not to lose, choose Heaven and not Hell." He says this to you right now - even as you read. I say it to you also as First Lady Buchanen always says to me, "God made you the best - now be the best!"

INSCRIPTIONS OF MY HEART

Biography

Kelly Price, the daughter of the late Elder Joseph Price and Evangelist Claudia Price is the 2nd of three children born and raised in Queens, NY. Under the watchful eye of her mother and the pastorate of her grandparents Bishop Jerome and Evangelist Joni Norman, Kelly was nurtured and developed spiritually by being taught the word of God and the importance of a sustained prayer life through the special prayer services her grandfather held weekly in addition to Sunday services and Bible study. It was there at an early age in Full Gospel Mission COGIC that the many gifts deeply rooted inside of her were watered and began to grow. It was there that her inner senses were awakened to the very real existence of God as more than just a higher power or an answer to a question "how did we all get here?" It was also there that the many gifts God planted inside of her were cultivated and began to grow.

At an early age, Kelly's musical talents began to dominate her life. While most babies have to be taken from the crib and calmed from crying in the middle of the night, Ms. Price's mother has been noted telling of the times when the entire house would be awakened at the sound of young Kelly singing out in her crib while the rest of the family tried to sleep. As a young child, Kelly knew that music was more than just something that happened on the radio, in church, or even during the commercials on TV. For her, it was a part of life that quickly became a necessity for life. She became emotionally dependent on the music inside of her and quickly learned how to use the music as an outlet to express what she was feeling, even when she couldn't speak about it. One day, after experiencing deep sadness from a book she read for a Black history project in school, Kelly wrote a song to express her unexplainable emotions. This was her first song. She was 7 years old.

Kelly sang on her first recording before the age of 10 and by the time she was 18, Kelly was recording and touring the world with multi-platinum pop diva, Mariah Carey. Always a quick study, Kelly watched and learned the intricacies of studio and production work and shortly after, began to expand into areas beyond background singing. It is these early years of her professional career that Kelly refers to as her formal education. While her classmates attended college to prepare for their careers, she went to work everyday and studied with the entertainment industry's best to prepare for what would soon be her own amazing career. During these years and beyond, Kelly has shared her multiple musical gifts with many artists and reached number one on Billboard's charts several times before anyone even knew what the girl behind the voice and the pen looked like. Throughout her career, Kelly has sang for, recorded with, toured with, written songs for, arranged and produced music for Mariah Carey, Aretha Franklin, Brian McKnight, Ben Tankard, Mary J Blige, Puff Daddy, Brandy, The LOX, Donnie McClurkin, The Williams Brothers, Faith Evans, Karen Clarke-Sheard, Yolanda Adams, MASE, Whitney Houston, Mary Mary, Notorious B.I.G., Richard Smallwood, R. Kelly, Eric Clapton, Wynona Judd, The Isley Brothers and the legendary Ronald Isley, to name a few. Though many record labels initially pursued Kelly as a recording artist, it was her connection with Isley and his relentless persistence that convinced her to begin to use her musical talents for herself, resulting in a formal alliance between Isley and Price that birthed her solo career with the album *Soul of a Woman* in 1998 that featured the number one smash women's anthem of the year "Friend of Mine," penned by Ms. Kelly Price. She would follow with the platinum success of *Mirror Mirror 2000*, *One Family—A Christmas Album* in 2002 and the critically acclaimed *Priceless* in 2003.

Out of the box, Ms. Price broke records by reaching Billboard's top spot twice with the same song and having achieved that initial number one victory with no music video on television. This had never been done by any artist since the format of music videos became the major marketing method by which record companies promote and sell music. Kelly also helped to usher in the rebirth of the Gospel sound in mainstream and R&B markets making the sound of a full voice acceptable among younger artists again. This, while also fighting a very real battle of imaging and acceptance in an industry that said "no one wants to look at a fat girl no matter how good she sounds."

Millions of albums later, this award-winning, Grammy-nominated singer, songwriter, producer, actress and now, author has only shown the beginning of who the world will come to know Kelly Price to be.

Kelly's life-long desire is to see people all over the world come into true freedom by understanding who they are, why they were created and how to press through anything that comes their way to make sure they fulfill their divine destinies.

It is her firm belief that this must be done by any means necessary and for her, this means GO! GO INTO THE WORLD! COMPEL PEOPLE EVERYWHERE TO COME. AND LEAD BY EXAMPLE! Kelly recently completed her first Gospel LP entitled *This is Who I Am* slated to release later this year on her newly established record label, EcclectiSounds Records.

It is through the efforts of this new life-inspired music and Kelly's *Inscriptions of My Heart* book series that this married mother of two desires to give people everywhere a greater understanding of who God isn't so they will no longer fear or resent Christianity.

Millions of albums later, this award-winning, Grammy-nominated, singer, songwriter, producer, actress and now author, has only begun to show the world the extraordinary woman it will come to know as Kelly Price.

Kelly's life desire is to see people all over the world come into true freedom by understanding who they are, why they were created and how to press through anything that comes their way to make sure they fulfill their divine destinies. It is her firm belief that this must be done by any means necessary and for her this means to GO!

GO INTO THE WORLD! COMPEL PEOPLE EVERYWHERE TO COME, AND LEAD BY EXAMPLE!

Kelly has recently completed her first Gospel LP entitled *This is Who I Am*, slated to release later this year on her newly established record label EcclectiSounds Records.

It is through the efforts of this new life-inspired music and the Inscriptions of My Heart book series, she is now authoring, that this married mother of two desires to give people everywhere a greater understanding of who God is - and who God isn't - so they will no longer fear or resent Christianity.